NAPOLEON'S
GRAND BRITISH HOLIDAY

NAPOLEON'S
GRAND BRITISH HOLIDAY

The Remarkable Story of Bonaparte
and His Time on the South Devon Coast

Mike Holgate

HALSGROVE

First published in Great Britain in 2015

Copyright © Mike Holgate 2015

British Library Cataloguing-in-Publication Data
A CIP record for this title is available from the British Library

ISBN 978 0 85704 260 6

HALSGROVE
Halsgrove House,
Ryelands Business Park,
Bagley Road, Wellington, Somerset TA21 9PZ
Tel: 01823 653777   Fax: 01823 216796
email: sales@halsgrove.com

Part of the Halsgrove group of companies
Information on all Halsgrove titles is available at: www.halsgrove.com

Printed in China by the Everbest Printing Co Ltd

CONTENTS

ACKNOWLEDGEMENTS

The author would like to extend his grateful thanks to members of the Torquay Library Local History Group, where, at a monthly meeting, the idea to commemorate the bicentenary of Napoleon Bonaparte's visit to the area as a prisoner of war was first discussed. My employer, Torquay Library kindly provided access to original copies of a London Sunday newspaper, *The News*, covering the four week period 30 July – 20 August 1815, which also included a round-up of eye-witness accounts, comment, letters and poems, culled from a range of daily newspapers, expressing varied views about the fallen emperor's reception and his ultimate fate. Historical information, biographical details and period illustrations were obtained from antiquarian books held by Torbay Library Services and the Internet Archive.

INTRODUCTION

The Battle of Waterloo in June 1815 finally brought peace to Europe, which had suffered over twenty years of warfare, inflicted by the 'Disturber of the World' – Napoleon Bonaparte (1769–1821). The self-crowned Emperor of France had been forced to abdicate in 1814, but executed a daring return from exile on the isle of Elba before his bid to regain power ended in a crushing defeat at the hands of the Duke of Wellington. Fleeing from the battlefield, 'Boney' found he was unwelcome in France, where the monarchy had been restored and Louis XVIII had branded him a 'rebel and traitor'. His plan to reach the sanctuary of America was foiled by a naval blockade; therefore, he somewhat optimistically applied to live amongst the enemy and instantly became Britain's most celebrated asylum seeker.

Brought to England in triumph by the Royal Navy, the appearance of Napoleon, on a warship anchored off the South Devon coast provided the area with an instant tourist attraction. Bonaparte had dismissed Britain as 'a nation of shopkeepers' but now inadvertently benefitted such traders when sightseers from all over the country flocked to the area around Torbay and Plymouth. Multitudes of people tried to catch a glimpse of the 'Great Thief of Europe' from a flotilla of small craft casting off from neighbouring coastal towns and villages. Although labelled 'the most infamous of criminals', surprisingly there was considerable admiration for Napoleon, which turned to sympathy when it was announced that he was to be banished to the inhospitable island of St Helena. Sections of the British press argued strongly that this move was illegal without a trial. Furthermore, as hostilities had ceased and Napoleon was no longer a head of state, they believed he was entitled to be released just like any common prisoner of war. The Duke of Cumberland, brother of the Prince Regent, was also disappointed with the government's decision to exile Napoleon Bonaparte, for, realizing that there was money to be made from the star attraction, the royal entrepreneur made a serious bid to take the military celebrity off the navy's hands and charge the public admission to see the prize exhibit in a cage!

Whilst compiling this book of contemporary eye-witness accounts, opinions, letters, songs and poems, the following quote from an obituary of the 'enlightened despot' gave advice on how to approach the subject in commemorating the bicentenary of Napoleon Bonaparte's enforced 'cruise' in the waters near my home in Devon:

The future historian will, if he cannot remove any of them, diminish the apparent bulk of the mass of crimes which have been heaped upon the character of Napoleon by a just arrangement; and if he must exhibit beneath them a character naked of any virtue, he will be able to trace the monster in morality thus displayed, to the same source as the splendid success of a military adventurer, and the magnificent authority of a military Sovereign.
(*St James Chronicle*, July 1821)

Mike Holgate
Torquay, December 2014

CHAPTER 1
The Rise and Fall of Napoleon

Boney met the Duke of Wellington
Way-aye-yah!
That day his downfall had begun
Jean Francois!

The Duke of Wellington, conqueror of Napoleon Bonaparte, accorded his enemy the utmost respect by acknowledging that his opponent was 'the best general of any age'. Of Italian descent, Napoleon was raised on the Mediterranean island of Corsica, which was conquered and became a

Facing the Enemy: Boney's cockerel is scared of John Bull's bulldog

Wellington: The Iron Duke   Napoleon quickly rose from military
                                         student to brigadier

region of France in the year he was born, 1769. Upon completing four years military education at the School of Brienne, his school certificate gave little indication of the fame he would achieve:

> *Character: submissive, mild, polite and obliging; Conduct: extremely regular; has always distinguished himself by his application to the mathematics. He knows his history and geography very tolerably; is very deficient in the politer exercises; will make an excellent seaman; worthy to enter the Military School of Paris.*

Overcoming his 'tolerable' knowledge of history and geography, Napoleon would become one of the greatest military leaders of modern times, overrunning much of Europe during his reign as the Emperor of France.

Quickly rising through the ranks during the French Revolution (1789–1799) when the monarchy was overthrown and a republic created in his adopted country, the soldier known throughout his meteorical career, affectionately at home and derisively abroad, as 'The Little Corporal'

Napoleon's supporters overthrow the Directory

attained the rank of brigadier at the age of twenty-one. Despite the violent turmoil and bloodshed within France, the country was simultaneously involved in military conflicts with other nations of Europe. Napoleon drove the British out of Toulon in 1793, then, three years later, defeated the Austrians and Sardinians to gain promotion as Commander-in-Chief of

The self-crowned Emperor of France

the Army of Italy. Initially, Napoleon supported the revolutionary movement and the newly-formed government of the First Republic known as the Directory, and in 1795, helped to suppress a royalist insurrection and was promoted to major general. However, in 1799, he seized power by forming a group which successfully overthrew the unpopular five-man Directory and replaced it by leading a three-man Consulate. He consolidated his position with an impressive victory in Italy against the Austrians at the Battle of Marengo (1800). Two years later, the country's leading politician appointed himself First Consul for life, then, in 1804, elevated himself to the title of Emperor. Napoleon infamously took the crown from the hands of Pope Pius VII in a lavish ceremony held at the Cathedral of Notre Dame in Paris.

The self-crowned emperor then reintroduced the aristocracy, largely wiped out by purges and executions during the bloody revolution, by bestowing crowns and titles on close members of his family as his empire expanded. Napoleon himself was also King of Italy, his stepson Eugene (by his marriage to first wife Josephine de Beauharnais), was appointed

The Bonaparte Brotherhood: (left to right)
Jerome, Lucien, Napoleon, Louis and Joseph

Napoleon led his army to victory in forty battles

governor of the same country, and his baby son, Napoleon II (from his second marriage to Marie Louise of Austria), the King of Rome, while Bonaparte's brothers were crowned: King Joseph of Spain, King Louis of Holland, King Jerome of Westphalia (a region of Germany), Prince Lucien of Canino (part of Italy), and his brother-in-law, Jerome Murat, became King of Naples (incorporating Corsica and Sardinia). During the period known as the Napoleonic Wars (1803–15), Bonaparte reached the pinnacle of his success defeating the Austrians and Russians at Ulm and Austerlitz (1805), the Prussians at Jena and Auerstadt (1806), the Russians at Friedland (1807) and the Austrians yet again at Wagram (1809). By 1810 Napoleon's brilliance on the battlefield and the political acumen that led him to be dubbed 'the enlightened despot' – with the introduction of social reform and a civil legal system known as the Napoleonic Code – ensured that he was presiding over the largest empire that had been witnessed since Roman times. Looking back on his career, Napoleon would summarise: 'My true glory is not to have won forty battles. Waterloo will erase the memory of so many victories. But what nothing will destroy, what will live forever, is my Civil Code.'

The Battle of Waterloo (1815) was to finally bring an end to Napoleon's long military and political career, though, inevitably, like the Roman Empire before it, the French suffered a series of major reversals of fortune leading up to that point, notably, the disastrous Russian campaign resulting in a retreat from snowbound Moscow (1812), and the rout by a coalition of Austrian, Prussian, Russian and Swedish forces at the Battle of Leipzig (1813). The self-crowned emperor's downfall continued when the allied forces captured Paris. As a condition of the subsequent Treaty of Fontainebleau, Napoleon was forced to abdicate and accept exile and sovereignty over the island of Elba in the Mediterranean. The following folk song emerged to chart Napoleon's descent from power and the final parting from his wife, Empress Marie Louise, described in the song as the 'royal whore', who returned to her native Austria with their son Napoleon II:

Boney's Abdication

Attend, ye sons of high renown
To these few words which I pen down:
I was born to wear a stately crown
And to rule a wealthy nation.
I am the man that beat Beaulieu,
And Wurmer's will did then subdue;
That great Archduke I overthrew,
On every plain my men were slain.
Grand traverse, too, I did obtain
And I got capitulation.

We chased them o'er the Egyptian shore
Where the Algerians lay all in their gore.
The rights of France for to restore
That had long been confiscated.
We chased them all through mud and mire
Till in despair my men did retire,
And Moscow town was set on fire.
My men were lost 'mid sleet and frost;
I never did take such a blast
Since the hour I was created.

To Leipzig Town my soldiers fled,
Mount Mark was strewn with the Prussian dead.
We marched them forth in inveterate streams
For to stop a bold invasion.
So fare thee well, my royal whore,
And offspring great whom I adore,
And may you reinstate that throne
That's torn away this very day.
These kings of me have made their prey
And that's caused my abdication.

Napoleon signs his abdication notice in Paris

'The Hundred Days' from March to June 1815, was to prove Napoleon Bonaparte's swansong. Conceding that, 'Power is my mistress. I have worked too hard at her conquest to allow anyone to take her away from me', he escaped from exile on Elba and was warmly welcomed back in France by the army, commanded by Marshal Ney, who, having previously deserted Napoleon at Fontainbleau in 1814 and pledged his loyalty to Louis XVIII, now rejoined Napoleon, after falsely promising the monarch he would bring the escapee 'back to Paris in an iron cage'. The recently installed king was forced to flee to Ghent, pursued by an invasion force intent on overrunning Belgium protected by an Allied army led by Field Marshall Arthur Wellesley, the Duke of Wellington. Napoleon left Paris in

Napoleon was exiled to Elba off the coast of Italy

June to join the army assembled in Belgium and defeated the Prussians at Ligny. Two days later, prior to the battle that would decide his personal fate and the future of Europe, he issued a stirring proclamation to his soldiers, drawing on the memories of glorious victories:

> *This day is the anniversary of Marengo and Friedland, which twice decided the destiny of Europe. After Austerlitz and Wagram we were too generous. We believed in the protestations and oaths of princes, to whom we left their thrones. Now, leagued together, they strike at the independence and sacred rights of France. Let us march forward and meet them. Are we not the same men? Soldiers! At Jena these Prussians were three to our one, at Montmirail six to our one... The Saxons, Belgians, Hanoverians, and soldiers of the Confederation of the Rhine, lament to have to use their arms on behalf of princes who are the enemies of justice, and destroyers of the rights of nations... Madness! One moment of prosperity has bewildered these Allies... Soldiers! Forced marches are before us, battles to be fought, dangers to be encountered; but, firm in resolution, victory must be ours. The honour and happiness of our country are at stake! And, in short, Frenchmen, the moment has arrived when we must conquer or die.*

The decisive battle of Napoleon Bonaparte's career took place near the Belgian village of Waterloo on 18 June. It was fought between his hastily recruited army of 72 000 men and the Duke of Wellington's Allied army of 68 000 (assembled from British, Dutch, Belgian and German forces). The outnumbered allies were fighting a losing battle until 45 000 Prussian reinforcements, who, following their recent defeat, had regrouped under their commander Field Marshall Gebhard Leberecht von Blucher, arrived

The Battle of Waterloo

Napoleon's Lament after The Battle of Waterloo
Extract from poem by J.W.P.

My Eagles are lost! And my warriors are dead!
My meteor-like glories are flown,
Like fancied felicity's dreams they are fled,
And with them – has vanished my throne!

The sun when he rose, saw their wings in the air,
In the trappings of Victory drest:
The sun, when he set, saw them sink in despair,
Unpitied – undreaded – unblest!

No more shall the tri-coloured standard unfurl'd
Triumphantly stream in the air:
Nor my Eagle, but lately the dread of the world,
The world with impunity dare.

My laurels are faded, no more will they bloom!
All their sweet recollections are past;
From my high-purpled greatness to meet such a doom,
Were in summer a wintery blast.

My sceptre now broken, my nod, which was fate,
Unheeded and harmless are shown!
Tho' the one's iron reign was saluted as great,
And the other was Jupiter's own.

Then farewell to Europe! And farewell to Gaul!
An asylum I seek o'er the wave,
From my Rise, and my triumphs, Reverses and Fall,
To meet with an undisturb'd grave.
(Morning Chronicle, 7 October 1815)

to rout the French. Even then, the result might have been very different as troops summoned to Napoleon's aid failed to arrive because the recipient, Marshal Grouchy, misread one word in a scribbled dispatch sent from the field. The phrase 'The battle is *begun*' was misinterpreted as 'The battle is *won*' and Grouchy spent the rest of the day six miles away at Wavre. In the aftermath of his greatest battle, the Duke of Wellington readily admitted that the victorious outcome was the 'nearest run thing you ever saw in your life'.

During the negotiations at Fontainebleau in 1814, Napoleon had declined a surprising invitation from Lord Castlereagh, Leader of the House of Commons, suggesting an alternative residence, which, was soon to gain renewed significance in the thoughts of the fallen emperor:

Why does not Napoleon, instead of going to Elba, come to England? He will be received in London with the greatest consideration, and he will obtain there a treatment infinitely preferable to exile on a wretched rock in the Mediterranean. He should not, however, make his retirement to England the object of negotiation, for that would entail too many delays, and provoke difficulties. But let him surrender himself without conditions; let him render this homage of esteem to an enemy which has bravely fought against him during ten years. He will be received in England with the profoundest respect, and he will learn that it is better worth his while to rely on English honour than on a treaty signed in the midst of circumstances such as at present exist.

CHAPTER 2

Bonaparte's Blockade

Boney went to Waterloo
Way-aye-yah!
There he got his overthrow
Jean Francois!

Napoleon Bonaparte fled from his homeland planning to seek refuge in America where his return to power had been greeted with joy in the press: 'Napoleon the Great is popular throughout America since his return from Elba and re-assumption of the throne, and he ought to be for the system of freedom he is now establishing'. In 1803, Napoleon had

Jack Tar settles with Boney

The Battle of New Orleans

funded his military ambitions by selling French territory in North America to the United States government raising $15million from the Louisiana Purchase. Seen in Europe as an extension of the Napoleonic Wars, America had declared war on Britain in June 1812 for a number of reasons including: trade restrictions created by the war in Europe; the continual impressment of American merchant sailors into the Royal Navy; and unresolved issues relating to the American Revolutionary War (1775–83) which brought about the country's independence. The 1812 War severely stretched the military and financial resources of Britain, which was simultaneously involved in the war with France. Late in 1814, a peace treaty between Britain and America was signed but, due to communication problems, was not enacted in time to prevent the British suffering a major defeat at the Battle of New Orleans (ironically, a city established by French colonists), in January 1815. This was the latest in a string of morale-boosting victories for the Americans, therefore, the war ended on a high note for a country celebrating victory in what they felt was their 'Second War of Independence'. The war inspired Francis Scott Key to write a poem which later formed the lyric for the American national anthem 'The Star Spangled Banner'. A verse from the poem perfectly describes the situation faced by Napoleon as he sailed from Rochefort hoping that nothing would prevent him from making a fresh start across the Atlantic:

> *On the shore dimly seen through the mists of the deep,*
> *Where the foe's haughty host in dread silence reposes,*
> *What is it that which the breeze, o'er the towering steep,*
> *As it fitfully blows, half conceals, half discloses?*
> *Now it catches the gleam of the morning's first beam,*
> *In full glory reflected now shines in the stream:*
> *'Tis the star spangled banner. O! long may it wave,*
> *O'er the land of the free and the home of the brave.*

Napoleon's dream of living 'in the land of the free and the home of the brave' was doomed. The British Admiralty received intelligence of the fugitive's plan to flee the country and lost no time in issuing a general signal:

> *The Lords Commissioners of the Admiralty having every reason to believe that Napoleon Bonaparte mediates his escape with his family to France to America, you are hereby required and directed, in pursuance of orders from their Lordships, signified to me by Admiral the Rt. Honourable Viscount Keith, to keep the most vigilant look-out for the purpose of intercepting him, and to make the strictest search of any vessel you may fall in with. ...*
> *If you should be so fortunate as to intercept him, you are to transfer him and his family to the ship you command and there keep him in careful custody and return to the nearest port in England, going into Torbay in preference to Plymouth, with all possible expedition, and on your arrival you are not to permit any communication with the shore.*

Eleven ships of the line formed the blockade of the port Rochefort in a bid to ensnare their celebrated military quarry. The prestigious prize was claimed by the *Bellerophon*, a 74 gun warship that her crew nicknamed *Billy Ruffian*. Built in 1782, she played a conspicuous part in the most famous sea battles of her era: the Battle of the Glorious First of June (1794) which was the opening action against Revolutionary France; the Battle of the Nile (1798) which halted Napoleon's eastern expansion; and the Battle of Trafalgar (1805) during which her captain was shot dead an hour before Nelson was mortally wounded. However, in the aftermath of the Battle of Waterloo, the *Bellerophon* achieved her crowning glory when Napoleon Bonaparte and his entourage surrendered to the ship's commander, Captain Frederick Maitland. Accompanying Bonaparte were his closest supporters: Count Henri-Gratien Bertrand, Grand Marshall of the Palace, his wife, Fanny and the couple's three children; Rene Savary the Duke of Rivigo, General Charles Lallemand, Baron Gaspard Gourgand, aide-de-camp to Bonaparte, Count Charles-Tristan de Montholon, his wife Albine and their child; Count Emmanuel de Las Cases, Counsellor of State, and his

Count Montholon   *Count Las Cases*

son; several other officers, a surgeon, and a suite of about forty loyal staff and servants.

The News (Sunday 30 July) published extracts from a letter submitted by an unidentified officer on board HMS *Cyrus* who had recorded particulars of the naval operation resulting in the detection and apprehension of Napoleon:

July 1: While within Isle of Dien, at anchor ... a boat came on board from HMS Bellerophon *with dispatches, announcing that Bonaparte had quitted Paris for some port in the Southward, intending to go to America; and requiring us to come down and assist her in the blockade of Rochefort. We immediately proceeded to Quiberon Bay to Admiral Hotham with this intelligence.*

July 12: Bellerophon *telegraphed us: 'Keep close off Balaine Lighthouse: Bonaparte is there endeavouring to escape. Examine every description of vessels closely for him. I have two of his generals, who have asked [permission] for the frigates to pass'.*

July 13: At 1.30pm, saw the Bellerophon *and* Slaney *some distance to leeward, with flags of truce at their mast-heads, and a chasse marée with a similar flag, so we had little doubt of Napoleon having surrendered, or being at least negotiating for that purpose.*

July 14: The Superb, Admiral Hotham, directed to us anchor within the Breton Passage, the more effectually to blockade it, and then passed on to Basque Roads to join the Bellerophon.

July 15: The Slaney *passed us, and telegraphed, 'For England, and with important dispatches'.*

July 16: We were recalled to this place, and found 'The Disturber of the World', whom we had been so anxiously looking for, safe on board the Bellerophon. *He was just returning from the latter ship from breakfasting* on board the *Superb* with the Admiral, who ordered the yards to be manned as a mark of respect.

We passed close to the **Bellerophon** *several times: Captain Maitland told us, 'I have got Bonaparte on board'… [Napoleon had] first sent out to Captain Maitland for permission to proceed to America in the frigates, which was refused; but an offer was made of referring him, if he came out, to the Admiral. He then asked for a brig, and afterwards for a schooner – requests equally inadmissible. Afterwards he formed the plan for going in two chasse marées out of the Breton Passage in the night, and being informed that this ship would intercept him, he replied, 'He would try, for we would not suspect such small vessels'. This determination was altered, probably by reflecting, that if taken prisoner he would have no claim on our generosity, while by throwing himself into our power, there might at least be some hope in setting up such a claim. He then surrendered after threatening to force his passage…*

On board the **Bellerophon**… *He acknowledged that England alone had ruined all his grand plans, and that but for her he would now be Emperor of the East as well as the West.*

In conversing with the Admiral, he said, 'I have given myself up to the English, but I would not have done so to any other of the Allied Powers. In surrendering to any of them I should be subject to the caprice and will of an individual: in submitting to the English, I place myself at the mercy of a nation'.

An anonymous officer on board *Bellerophon* gave details to the press of a seemingly remarkable change of attitude towards war by Napoleon:

He professes his intentions (if allowed to reside in England) to adopt the English customs and manners, and declares that he will never meddle in politics any more. The army which left Paris, and united with others on the Loire, wanted him to join and resume his title, but he refused to do so. He declares that not another 'goutte de sang' [drop of blood] shall be shed on his account. Fortunate, indeed, it would have been if he had really been of this opinion some years back.

Napoleon echoed these peaceful intentions in a letter addressed to the Prince Regent, ruler of Britain due to the mental incapacity of his father 'Mad' King George III:

> *Royal Highness,*
> *A victim to the factions which divide my country, and to the enmity of the great powers of Europe, I have terminated my political career, and I come, like Themistocles* [Athenian general and politician who was ostracised and exiled in Argos c471 BC], *to throw myself upon the hospitality of the British Nation. I place myself under the protection of its laws, which I claim from your Royal Highness as the most powerful, the most constant, and the most generous of my foes.*

Captain Frederick Maitland ordered the asylum seeker's request to be hastily conveyed to England by HMS *Slaney* along with an explanatory letter of his own actions addressed to the Secretary of the Admiralty:

> *Sir,*
> *For the information of the Lords Commissioners of the Admiralty, I have to acquaint you that the Count Las Cases and General Lallemand this day came on board His Majesty's Ship under my command, with a proposal from Count Bertrand for me to receive on board Napoleon Bonaparte, for the purpose of throwing himself on the generosity of the Prince Regent. Conceiving myself authorised by their Lordships' secret order, I have acceded to the proposal, and he is to embark on board this ship tomorrow morning. That no misunderstanding might arise, I have explicitly explained to Count de Las Cases that I have no authority whatever for granting terms of any sort, but that all I can do is to carry him and his suite to England, to be received in such manner as His Royal Highness may deem expedient.*
> *At Napoleon Bonaparte's request, and that their Lordships may be in possession of the transaction at as early a period as possible, I despatch the* Slaney *(with General Gourguad, his aide de camp), directing Captain Sartorius go put into the nearest port, and forward this letter by his first*

Count Bertrand   *General Gourgard*

Lieutenant, and shall in compliance with their Lordships' orders proceed to Torbay, and await such directions as the Admiralty may think proper to give.

Enclosed, I transmit a copy of the letter with which General Gourguad, is charged to His Royal Highness the Prince Regent, and request that you will acquaint their Lordships' that the General informs me, he is entrusted with further particulars, which he is anxious to communicate to His Royal Highness.

The messages referred to by Captain Maitland were summarised in an aide-memoire in which the former Emperor stated that his representative, General Gourgaud, on arrival in England, was to seek an audience with the Prince Regent and present the following highly optimistic options:

If HRH sees no objections to granting me passports, to go to the United States, it would be my intention to go there. But I do not desire to go to any other colony. If I cannot go to America, I wish to stay in England, assuming the name of Muiron or Doroc. In England I would like to live in a country house about ten to twelve leagues from London, after arriving strictly incognito. I would need a house large enough for my staff. I ask to keep away from London where I do not think the Government would like me to live. If the Government intends to provide me with a superintendent, he must not be a jailer but a man of quality and honour.

Instead of considering himself fortunate that the frigate he was sailing on had not been blown out of the water or that he was not transported to England clapped in irons, the deluded former emperor and his entourage were granted comfortable accommodation on board their floating prison, forcing the ship's officers and crew to sleep on deck during the ten day voyage to England. Despite the inconvenience caused by the presence of their foreign 'guests', a source from the *Bellerophon* disclosed that, during the voyage from France to England, Napoleon became a popular figure with the officers and crew as he 'walked on the poop and quarter deck, conversed with the seamen, and affected great gaiety and unconcern. In short, such is the talent of this "Child and Champion of Jacobinism", that before they arrived at their destination, he was considered by all on board as a "devilish good fellow."' Incredibly, in view of the heavy taxation and large number of casualties suffered by the country during the Napoleonic Wars, the sailors' favourable view of the perpetrator was to be endorsed by the huge crowds of people who welcomed the presence of the celebrated prisoner upon the *Bellerophon*'s arrival in Torbay. Despite denunciations in the Tory press, including *The Times, The Courier* and *Morning Herald*, that fully supported Prime Minister Lord Liverpool and the government's hard line over the fate of Napoleon, a more liberal view was expressed in *The News*:

Of the crimes and cruelties imputed to NAPOLEON we shall never become the defenders. They were all of the same nature which, have been committed by ambitious, successful men, from time immemorial. We now consider him as politically dead, and therefore are far more inclined to bring to our recollection his wonderful talents which made him what he was, than his bad deeds which have made him what he is. A generous man seeks not the

The officers and crew considered their passenger to be a 'Devilish good fellow'

destruction nor the degradation of his enemy - he is satisfied with his submission. But it is said that BONAPARTE'S submission was not made until he was compelled to it, and therefore that he is not entitled to receive any benefit from it... There is something generous in human nature which inclines us always to consider fallen greatness with pity. When we therefore view the captive NAPOLEON walking the quarter-deck of a British man of war, anxiously waiting the determination of our Government, as to the place of his future imprisonment, we cannot help recurring to the man, who, at Vienna, imposed laws on the Emperor of AUSTRIA, who did the same to the King of PRUSSIA at Berlin, and the same to the Emperor of RUSSIA at Tilsit – to him before whom the greatest have trembled – the creator of Kings, and the dispenser of Kingdoms.

(*The News*, 30 July 1815)

CHAPTER 3
The Bonaparte Invasion

Boney went a-cruising
Way-aye-yah!
Aboard the Billy Ruffian
Jean Francois!

With the *Bellerophon* anchored off the Devon coast, a local newspaper noted the irony of the manner in which Napoleon Bonaparte had finally reached Britain – not as a victorious military leader, but as a submissive captive:

Britain prepared for a French Invasion

The Usurper of the Throne of France, the Tyrant of Europe, the once invincible Bonaparte, is safely arrived in this kingdom; but not, as he had once fondly promised himself, at the head of a victorious army to ravage this country with fire and sword – to levy contributions on the merchants and bankers of our metropolis – and to despoil the Bank of England of its bullion! No! Thanks to the noble Wellington, and to our brave army under his command, he is now shorn of his laurels - driven from post to post – and at length, forced to seek refuge, as a PRISONER, on board a British man of war; depending for protection on the known humanity and liberality of the British government! How is the mighty fallen! The country to which he always openly avowed the most invincible hatred – to that government, of which he was ever lavish in his abuse - and to that Throne which he employed his servile Press to insult – he now becomes a humble petitioner, flattering himself, that by their influence, he will escape that condign punishment his conduct has so richly merited... But we will ask, ought not some atonement be made to the ashes of those brave heroes, whose lives have been sacrificed to the cruelty and ambition of this demon in human shape? How many widows and orphans and parents are there in this country, whose cheeks are still red with the tears for fathers, husbands, or children slain, through the traitorous villainy of this man?

(Trewman's Exeter Flying Post, 26 July 1815)

Napoleon's ambitious plans to invade Britain had been wrecked by British sea power. As the *Bellerophon* sailed into Torbay, where the Channel Fleet had utilised the sheltered anchorage during the prolonged years of war, Napoleon observed an unmanned fort on the cliffs of Berry Head. It had been built to defend the expected attack by the French, but the home defences had been rendered redundant as the French had been forced to abandon their designs on this island by the superiority of the Royal Navy. National hero Admiral Lord Horatio Nelson had scuppered Napoleon's Egyptian Campaign, where he had attempted to open up a route to take India from the British, at the Battle of the Nile (1798), and inflicted a damaging defeat, at the cost of his own life, during the Battle of Trafalgar (1805). When Napoleon obtained his first close-up view of the English

The Death of Nelson at Trafalgar

coastline the former emperor reportedly exclaimed: 'Enfin viola ce beau pays! – [At length here is this fine country] – adding that he had only seen it from Calais and Boulogne, where the only landmark visible to him was the white cliffs of Dover. Bonaparte was to spend a total of fifteen days off the Devon coast sailing into Torbay at 4am on Tuesday, 24 July, Napoleon viewed the surrounding countryside and recognised similarities to his previous residence in exile: 'What a beautiful country. It very much resembles Porto Ferrajo, in Elba'.

The unannounced appearance of HMS *Bellerophon*, caused a sensation at Brixham, Paignton and Torquay overlooking Torbay. The ship was soon surrounded with a flotilla of boats and yachts putting out to sea with sightseers from the neighbouring towns of Dartmouth, Teignmouth, Dawlish, Starcross, Exmouth, Exeter and Sidmouth. *Flindell's Western Luminary* commented on interviews with 'several gentlemen from Exeter' who made the trip to Torquay to view the imported tourist attraction:

Napoleon walking the deck on Bellerophon

Multitudes are flocking to the coast to see the ship; and many gentlemen have gone off and sailed round her, but no-one, that we hear of, has been admitted on board, though some have been alongside. Bonaparte we are told, walks the deck freely, and sometimes talks to the sailors. The officers treat him with great politeness. ... From the manner in which Captain Maitland appears to be waiting instructions, we fear the Bellerophon *will be off as soon as he receives them, without landing her prisoner here, to gratify the anxious curiosity of the neighbourhood.*

Captain Thomas Bond, R.N., recorded his experience in a letter sent on the 29 July from Torbay to his brother, Captain, later Rear-Admiral Francis Godolphin Bond, then residing a few miles along the coast at Starcross:

Did you see that scoundrel and murderer Bonaparte when in Torbay?... What will they do with him? I know what they ought, that of hanging

him... If we cannot effect this by law... do not let us degrade ourselves in
paying homage to this monster in human shape that we do. He now
continually plays the Emperor, and so he'll continue, while we are such
fools.

(Reproduced in *Torquay Directory*, 21 July 1915)

Captain Bond's view of Napoleon as a 'scoundrel and murderer' was not universally shared. *The News*, 6 August, reported a more sympathetic attitude extended to a fallen hero by the hordes of admiring sightseers: 'Bonaparte is treated by the immense crowds who come to see him, with that respect which the English are ever inclined to pay to misfortune, however merited. The sailors in particular view him with the greatest commiseration. They adopt a curious mode to give an account to the anxious spectators in the boats of his movements. They write in chalk on a board which they exhibit, a short account of his different occupations – "At breakfast" – "In the cabin with Captain Maitland" – "Writing with his officers" – "Going to dinner" – "Coming upon deck"'.

The News commented upon the scene stirred by the presence of Napoleon: 'Never was seen such a sight in Torbay. There are ladies and gentleman from 60 to 70 miles distant and upwards arriving this morning; never was such a concourse of people seen'. Many visitors arrived in Torbay too late to catch a glimpse of the great tourist attraction as the *Bellerophon* weighed anchor at 4 o'clock in the morning of 26 July, and set sail bound for Plymouth where the ship arrived in the Sound later that day at 4 o'clock in the afternoon.

Further correspondence from Plymouth published in the same newspaper observed that Napoleon appeared to sense the historic significance of this port of call where Francis Drake had famously assembled his fire-ships to thwart the King of Spain in 1588: 'He often looks through his glass at Mount Edgecombe, perhaps with the same view as the Duke of Medina Coeli, who, when hovering off Plymouth Sound, with the Spanish Armada, marked it out as his own, should the invasion prove successful'. The opening chaotic scenes that greeted Napoleon in Plymouth Sound were described in another letter:

On the arrival of the Bellerophon, *74, Hon. Captain Maitland, in Plymouth Sound, on Wednesday last, having on board Napoleon Bonaparte and suite, the* Euretas *and* Briton *frigates, then lying in the Sound, were immediately ordered to anchor near her, and six gunboats, with a lieutenant and eight men each, ordered to be continually rowing round her, to prevent any communication; so very strict are they, that no boat whatever (except the Admiral's) is permitted to come within the frigates or guard-boats, stationed about a cable's length distant round the* Bellerophon, *not even to lay to; and no distinction made to Captains and Officers in the Navy. Immense numbers of people have made efforts to get a nearer view, and have as often been peremptorily ordered off, or fired at.*

(*The News*, 6 August 1815)

Lieutenant John Bowerbank recorded Napoleon's reaction to the sound of warning shots being fired over the crowded vessels besieging the *Bellerophon*:

On anchoring in Plymouth Sound, two frigates, the Eurotas *and* Liffey, *were immediately stationed one on each side of us, and several guard boats commenced rowing round the ship. These proceedings did not long escape the notice of Bonaparte, who requested to know the reason of such precautions. After dinner he made his appearance, standing for some time on the gangway. Several boats had collected round us to whom he bowed, reconnoitring them as usual through his glass. He looked pale and dejected, and said but little. As it grew dark, the guard boats being unable to prevent the boats which still lingered round the ship from breaking through the limits assigned, they made frequent discharges of musketry. The sound of this greatly discomposed him, and he sent Bertrand to Captain Maitland, requesting that he would if possible prevent a repetition.*

By Monday, 31 July, a correspondent noted that the navy were experiencing great difficulty in keeping back the boatloads of sightseers besieging the *Bellerophon*:

Sightseers in small boats surround the Bellerophon *in Plymouth Sound*

The boats get within 30 yards of the Bellerophon, *and Bonaparte is seen at the gangway for 20 minutes at a time. He leaves the cabin and walks to the quarter deck and gangways while the cloth is laying for dinner, On Sunday, the weather clearing up, which had been unfavourable during the whole of Saturday, the Sound was again covered with an immense number of boats, and the pressure was so great, that the guard-boats, with extreme difficulty, kept them a few yards only from the ship. As the time for the appearance of Bonaparte drew nigh (a quarter before six) the exertion of the boats to get a 'good berth' produced no small confusion. ... When Bonaparte appeared, the innermost boats touched the side. A number of distinguished personages were observed in the men of war's boats in the inside, under the ship's ladder. The same scene, with little variation, took place on Monday, except that the number of boats had increased so much on both sides of the ship that the guard-boats were rendered useless, and the sides of the ship touched in every part. Bonaparte, as usual, appeared at a quarter to six on the larboard gangway – bowed – remained three minutes, and then went over to the starboard side, where he remained six or seven minutes. There were 1500 in the Sound, all crammed with spectators. It is supposed that there were not less than 10,000 persons round the* Bellerophon *this evening. Bonaparte stood on the gangway about half an hour, between six and seven o'clock.*

(*The News*, 6 August 1815)

Midshipman George Home revealed details of how some crew members were punished after playing a practical joke on people in the boats swarming around the *Bellerophon*:

If we could judge from the enormous rush that was made from every part of the country to Plymouth Sound to get a single glance of the hero of Marengo and Lodi Bridge, he must have conceived that he was as much admired by the English as by his own beloved French. The Sound was literally covered with boats; the weather was delightful; the ladies looked as gay as butterflies; bands of music in several of the boats played favourite French airs, to attract, if possible, the Emperor's attention, that they might get a sight of him, which, when effected, they went off, blessing themselves that they had been so fortunate. All this did not escape the eagle eye of Napoleon, and he showed no disinclination to gratify the eager spectators, by frequently appearing at the gangway, examining the crowd with his pocket-glass; and frequently, as a pretty face gazed at him with bewitching curiosity, he

The hero of Marengo and Lodi Bridge is cheered by his army

showed his fine white teeth, lifted the little three-cocked hat nearly off his broad and commanding forehead for he never wholly uncovered, bowed and smiled with evident satisfaction.

The signal for the Emperor's being on deck was the officers uncovering [their heads]. No sooner was this ceremony noticed, than the rush from without took place and the screaming and swearing commenced, which was very considerably heightened upon one occasion by a plan of some of our wise-headed young gentlemen. Being in want of amusement, they bethought them of priming the fire-engine, which happened to be standing on the poop, and after clapping a relay of hands ready to ply it to advantage, we uncovered and waited the approach of the boats. No sooner were they within reach than off went the waterspout, which fell 'alike on the just and the unjust' for both the dockyard men and the spectators who came within its compass got a good ducking. This prank created an infernal confusion, and our trick having been twigged by the first lieutenant, the chief actors in this notable exploit were ordered up to the masthead to enjoy their frolic for a few hours, which evidently much gratified the unfortunate sufferers from the effects of the operation.

The *Bellerophon* received new orders and left Plymouth with her imperious passenger on 4 August and made for Berry Head, off Brixham in Torbay. *Flindell's Western Luminary*, Exeter, recorded, 'The exhibition of this fascinating monster, Bonaparte, in Plymouth Sound, closed on Friday last, we are indebted to the kindness of friends for the following accounts of the show':

On Friday, the Bellerophon *got under way about one o'clock; and not having a satisfactory view of him, I went in a boat with a few other gentlemen, and followed the ship 'till she was some distance outside the breakwater. All this time he did not show himself: and, as the ship was working out, I take it for granted he was not on the quarter deck. However, as there was but one guard-ship rowing astern (the others being employed towing the ship, there being just a light air), we frequently ran up pretty near to her, and in consequence of two ladies who had embarked on board*

HMS Bellerophon *in Torbay with the cliffs of Berry Head in the background*

a shore boat, under the idea that having no gentlemen with them, they would be suffered to approach nearer the vessel, and who seemed most anxious to see the renowned prisoner she had on board, they frequently standing on the thwarts of the boat, and waving their handkerchiefs, he at last made his appearance at the stern cabin of the window, evidently for the purpose of satisfying their curiosity. He held his hand out of the window, and inclined it downwards, as if he was resting on his elbows, without his hat being on, which gave us a complete view of his face and head, which is very bald on the top, but the hair on the sides being suffered to grow long, we could perceive it was combed across. He stayed about a minute and then retired. We followed him until he got within a short distance of Penlee Point; but he did not show again. Indeed, I did not expect it, for in a short time after he looked out of the window, he drew the curtains of the cabin windows; when I remarked, that it was decidedly done to let us know that the Lion was no more to be seen. There appeared to be rather a bustle in the cabin, as if they were packing up for the intended removal into the Northumberland.

The *Bellerophon* anchored off Berry Head waiting for a supply vessel to arrive with provisions, then transferred Napoleon Bonaparte and selected members of his retinue to HMS *Northumberland*, the vessel tasked with carrying out the government's decision to send Bonaparte on the long voyage into exile on the inhospitable isle of St Helena in the South Atlantic. *The News*, 20 August, published some observations of the transfer of Napoleon by an unnamed officer on board the *Northumberland* in the following extract from a letter written on the day of sailing, 8 August 1815:

> *Lord Keith joined us off Torbay, when we received the celebrated General of the day. … There was a commanding majesty in his appearance, while he continued in the boat, which struck me as well represented me in the prints; but on his entre on the quarter deck, I thought the majesty of the character decreased. Bertrand acceded first – Napoleon followed. I was breathless with expectation. The Guard received him as a General. He was clad in a green coat, white facings, red collar, waistcoat, breeches, and stockings white, with a formidable cocked hat. He walked [with his head] uncovered to the after port of the quarter deck. He bowed to each individual, asked twenty questions, and appeared to smile with approbation at the reception he met with. He ate a most hearty dinner, came out afterwards, and requested the band to play 'God Save the King' and 'Rule Britannia'.*

The above letter ended with a query from two aggrieved passengers bound for St Helena, Count and Countess Bertrand: 'I have had a great deal of conversation with Madame Bertrand and with the Count; they are anxious to learn the sentiments of the English nation regarding their [government's] conduct'. An editorial in *The News* made clear their admiration for Napoleon and their view on what they perceived to be the unjust manner in which the celebrated prisoner of war and his supporters had been treated:

> *Our sentiments on the forced deportation of this extraordinary man have been openly and fully expressed in our proceeding numbers. It is indeed to*

be regretted for the honour of our country, that at a period when the name of England stands so high in military glory, advantage should not have been taken of the opportunity which his surrender, to place it equally above contradiction in the renown of magnanimity and forbearance. That some risk, would have attended this proceeding, we are ready to admit – but a certain portion of risk seems necessary in the constitution of all great actions, and here the risk was not so great (for he might have been watched) as to counterbalance the reputation… The behaviour of the officers and crew of the Bellerophon *is a proof of this. They were incapable of insulting over the fallen fortunes of a man who once gave laws to the greater part of the civilised world… If we take into consideration his exemplary emperance, his early rising, his simplicity of dress, his dignity of manner, his prodigious and incredible energy in the Cabinet, and in the field, his ardent love of literature, his undaunted courage, his promptitude of conception and rapidity of execution; if we can contemplate the unparalleled celerity and extent of his conquests, and call to mind the circumstances of his having effected the subjugation of Continental Europe before he had attained the age of forty: we shall not be surprised that all the Monarchs of Europe dread the very sound of his name. He has truly said posterity will judge him, and judge him justly… When some of the free passages of the English newspapers were read to Bonaparte, or rather when the Countess Bertrand, upon coining to them, suddenly stopped her reading, being unwilling to offend him by the epithets therein lavished on him, Bonaparte desired her to proceed, 'It is posterity, Madam, that will judge me justly; these people speak of what they do not understand'.*

The euphoria of the Duke of Wellington's victory at the Battle of Waterloo and the subsequent apprehension and transportation to England of Europe's formidable enemy dubbed the 'Disturber of the World' had been made evident in a popular song of the day:

Despite the popular sentiment expressed in the song that the capture of Napoleon Bonaparte had brought 'Peace to all Europe', the majority of the general public who made the journey to Devon appeared to be sympathetic to the plight of the deposed leader. Lieutenant John Bowerbank was

Napoleon: 'Posterity will judge me justly'

amazed at the scenes of adulation he had witnessed in Torbay, where the nation's enemy had received a rapturous reception from the swarms of spectators:

> *Bonaparte, frequently bowing... appeared pleased with their eagerness to see him, repeated, as did his officers: 'How very curious these English are!' I was, indeed, surprised at not hearing a disrespectful or abusive word*

Huzza! For John Bull, for England Huzza!

Huzza! For John Bull!

Written by Mr Parry

Gather round, good neighbours, I've news to disclose,
That will make you all merry, I'm sure,
John Bull's greatest torment, and worst of his foes,
Is now in his power, quite safe and secure:
Huzza! For John Bull, for England Huzza!
What a feather 'twill be in Gaffa Bull's cap,
To give Peace to all Europe, by taking a Nap!

That John is a Lion in Battle, we know,
But John is a Lamb when the conflict is o'er,
And what more could his honour more strikingly shew,
Than to see Bonaparte his protection implore.
Huzza! For John Bull, for England Huzza!
What a feather 'twill be in Gaffa Bull's cap,
To give Peace to all Europe, by taking a Nap!

John swore a small oath, that without more to do,
He would march into France, and there end the war:
He did so we know, and at famed Waterloo,
John hurled the proud foe from his blood-stained car
Huzza! For John Bull, for England Huzza!
What a feather 'twill be in Gaffa Bull's cap,
To give Peace to all Europe, by taking a Nap!

Napoleon oft said that to England he'd come,
And make us poor devils acknowledge his power;
He came to Torbay, without trumpet or drum,
But found the Grapes of Old England were sour!
Huzza! For John Bull, for England Huzza!
What a feather 'twill be in Gaffa Bull's cap,
To give Peace to all Europe, by taking a Nap!

(Lancaster Gazette, 19 August 1815)

51

Bonaparte on board the Bellerephon *off Plymouth, 1816*

escape from anyone. On the contrary the spectators generally took off their hats when he bowed. I have reason to believe that he himself expected, and most justly, a very different reception.

Similarly, the Editor of a Cornish newspaper, published in Truro, found reports of Bonaparte's reception and the behaviour of people who surrounded the *Bellerophon*, hard to believe:

As Englishmen we could not help but be ashamed at the baby-like curiosity that has been displayed in order to get a glimpse of this modern day Bajazet. We thought that we did but perform a common act of justice in exonerating the loyalty *of these wonder-mongers from impeachment, although, at the* expense *of their* intellect. *Well authenticated accounts have, however, shown us that we were deceived …. a considerable portion of the people who were in* Plymouth Sound, *took off their hats and cheered the tyrant the moment he appeared upon deck; and this was done, says a respectable paper (the* Plymouth Dock Telegraph), *'apparently with the view of soothing his fallen fortunes, and treating him with respect and consideration'!!*

(*Royal Cornwall Gazette*, 12 August 1815)

In a letter written on 7 August, a Plymouth correspondent also criticised well-wishers who had travelled long distances to see the 'monster' and proposed harsh measures for a group of supporters who had attempted to mount a legal challenge as a device to allow Napoleon Bonaparte to remain in England :

It was high time that Bonaparte should be moved from this neighbourhood, for it is shocking to see the court and attention that was paid to him; but don't blame the westcountrymen upon that score; his greatest admirers and adulators have come from every part of the country, even from Northumberland and Scotland: but what is to be said for the men who wished to screen such a monster under the Habeas Corpus Act? The least punishment that they deserve, in my opinion, and the best, would be to send them to St Helena with their friend.

(*The Times*, 10 August 1815)

CHAPTER 4
Celebrity Asylum Seeker

Boney sought asylum
Way-aye-yah!
England chose to banish him
Jean Francois!

Although the government quickly made it known to the press that Napoleon's future lay abroad in exile, a debate developed as to whether Napoleon Bonaparte's fate should be decided by the courts. A correspondent calling himself 'Probus', poured scorn on the prisoner's

Boney sentenced to death for 'Setting the World in an Uproar'

claims for asylum and insisted that he should be prosecuted for his crimes. His argument was outlined in a series of letters to the editor of *The Times*:

> *I cannot but think, that the age will be forever disgraced, and the cause of justice will endure a fatal shock, if Napoleon Bonaparte be not brought to* solemn *trial, and to* public execution...
>
> *What punishment can be just, if the condemning him to death be cruel? He has, for a long succession of years, deluged Europe in blood, to gratify his own mad vanity, his insatiable and furious ambition. It is calculated, that every* minute *he has reigned, has cost the life of a human being... Some hypocrites, and perhaps some idiots, may exclaim against the cruelty of thus persecuting a fallen enemy... The misfortunes of a generous enemy are to be respected. The fair chances of war create not the slightest ground for haughtiness or insolence: but it is mere imbecility of intellect to apply these principles in favour of robbers and murderers. For my own part I have always viewed Napoleon Bonaparte in this light.*
>
> (*The Times*, 26 July 1815)

Does the true history of Napoleon Bonaparte entitle him to use the impudence of writing to the Prince Regent? Certainly not. Educated at the expense, and by the liberality of Louis XVI, he set out in life as an ungrateful Rebel and Traitor. By marrying the cast-off mistress of another Traitor, and by firing on the citizens of Paris, he recommended himself to military preferment. As a General, he has always shown ability in the field, though with that diversity of fortune which leaves his reputation in the second line; but his military talents have been

Napoleon was branded a 'rebel and a traitor' in France

uniformly devoted to the furtherance of schemes of the most abominable iniquity that history has to record. A series of base intrigues led him to the easy usurpation of the Imperial title, a title, which as we never acknowledged it, can in no respect alter his relative situation, as to us. We have only to regard him as a military adventurer, who in the course of his career has violated towards us all decency, all honour, all sense of right and wrong. The latter part of that career has consisted of a most shameless attempt to place himself at the head of France and other countries in alliance with us, in violation of the terms on which his life had once been spared. By our exertions, this scheme of unexampled perjury and treason was defeated. Proclaimed a rebel and an outlaw in his own country he flies to us for protection. It would be insulting common sense to ask whether we are bound to treat him in any other way than any other thief or murderer is treated when he gives himself up into the hands of justice?

(*The Times*, 29 July 1815)

Capel Lofft, a constitutional lawyer and fervent admirer of Napoleon, submitted a letter to the editor of the *Morning Chronicle* contending that it was illegal to banish Bonaparte abroad without a trial. Referring to the Habeas Corpus Act of the second Magna Charta, covering 'All persons within the realm of England, which includes the adjoining seas, are temporary subjects if aliens, or permanent if natural born', he outlined his case:

Though not on British soil, he is within the British law. If at Plymouth, he is in a British county... I am of the opinion that deportation or transportation, or relegation, cannot legally exist in this country, except where the law expressly provides it on trial and sentence...

[Napoleon] voluntarily came on board [Bellerophon]; Captain Maitland received him agreeably, as the Captain understands, to secret orders. If he is debarred of all communication and correspondence, and forbidden to land, this must be by some order and for some purpose. And the Writ of Habeas Corpus is the legal mode of investigating, as to all persons whether their liberty be legally or illegally restrained, and all

Captain Frederick Lewis Maitland

restraint of liberty is illegal, of which, the legality is not clearly and strictly proved. I know of no law of ours which supports such conduct, as is asserted to have already taken place, and to be further determined.

However, a writ of habeas corpus, requiring those detaining Napoleon to produce his body before a judge with a view to ordering his release, was not forthcoming as the government contended that a prisoner of war was not a bona fide resident and therefore, outside the scope of the law.

Not to be outdone, Capel Lofft colluded with a Mr McKenrot, a legally trained litigant with mental health issues who would end his days in Bedlam. Born in London, of German extraction, McKenrot obtained a minor legal appointment in Tortola, an island in the Lesser Antilles. Whilst residing there, he gained notoriety by picking a quarrel with Admiral Sir Alexander Cochrane, accusing him of cowardice in the face of the enemy for not attacking a French squadron weaker than his own at the beginning of 1815. Admiral Cochrane responded against this blatant attempt to blacken his character by bringing an action for libel against McKenrot in London.

On 14 June 1815, the defendant obtained permission from the court to call three witnesses: Admiral Willaumez, the commander of the aforesaid enemy squadron; Jerome Bonaparte – younger brother of Napoleon – who was on board the same vessel; and finally the Emperor of France, Napoleon Bonaparte, who had made a triumphant return from exile on Elba. With such an absurd request for unobtainable witnesses, the case would have remained a dead letter, had it not been for the Battle of Waterloo, and the unexpected availability of a key witness, sitting on the *Bellerophon* in British

57

territorial waters. With Capel Lofft's encouragement, McKenrot attempted to serve a subpoena on Napoleon. This action meant that Admiral Lord Keith, commanding the Channel and Atlantic squadrons, that included the *Bellerophon*, would be obliged to comply with the order of the court and deliver up the required witness. If the legal ruse worked, the government's plan to send their prisoner into exile would have to be postponed as the hearing was set for November, and once ashore, the asylum seeker's claims for permanent residency would be strengthened. A cat and mouse game ensued as McKenrot travelled post-haste to Plymouth and scoured the area desperately trying to serve the subpoena before the *Northumberland* set sail for St Helena with Napoleon.

During these latest legal developments, Lord Keith reported to the First Lord of the Admiralty, Lord Melville:

I must be particularly vigilant, for the 'General' and his suite are convinced that once they step foot on shore, no power on earth can bring them back again. They are determined to disembark. It is all they talk of and they are becoming aggressive.

On 2 August, Lord Melville replied to Lord Keith warning him that legal shenanigans were afoot and 'ON NO ACCOUNT to permit Bonaparte to come on shore':

In some of the newspapers a notion is held out that he may be brought out of the ship by a writ of Habeas Corpus. The serious public inconvenience and danger which would arise from such an occurrence, even though he may not escape and be remanded by a judge as a prisoner-of-war, renders it indispensably our duty to prevent it.

Arriving in Plymouth on 4 August and booking accommodation at the King's Arms Tavern, near Plymouth Dockyard, McKenrot immediately began his quest to serve the subpoena on Napoleon or his guardian, Lord Keith. Calling on the superintendent of the dockyard, Sir John Duckworth, McKenrot asked for permission to serve the writ on Napoleon. Duckworth explained that he did not have the authority to comply with such a request as the Emperor was the responsibility of Lord Keith. McKenrot hastened to his lordship's residence and was informed by Lady Keith that her husband was probably on board one of the ships of the squadron anchored in the Sound. McKenrot continued his search by hiring a boat and excitedly waved the writ as he spotted Napoleon in his cabin through the stern window of the *Bellerophon*. However, this was as close as McKenrot got to his quarry, as the men on the guard ships surrounding the vessel warned him to stay clear. Meanwhile, Lord Keith had received a communication from the secretary of his household that McKenrot was in hot pursuit, and he immediately took steps to avoid a meeting and took off from the flag ship *Tonnant* in a pinnace. Outmanoeuvred and frustrated in his efforts to track down the elusive Admiral, McKenrot delivered the following letter to his lordship's residence later that day:

I arrived this morning from London with a writ issued by the Court of King's Bench to subpoena Napoleon Bonaparte as a witness in a trial impending in that Court.

I was extremely anxious of waiting on your Lordship most humbly to solicit your permission to serve such process on your said prisoner: but unfortunately could not obtain any admittance into your presence, neither at your own house nor on board HMS Tonnant, *where your lordship was said to be.*

I humbly entreat your lordship to consider that an evasion to give due facility to the execution of my process would amount to a high contempt against the honourable Court from whence it issues, and that under the continuances of such

Admiral Lord Keith

circumstances, I shall be under the painful necessity of making my return accordingly.

Leaving the issue to your Lordship's discretion, I shall return here until tomorrow night; but to remove all doubts from your mind, I beg to enclose a copy of the writ for your perusal.

Having delivered the above notification, McKenrot returned to the harbour and once more made for the *Tonnant*, but the Admiral saw him coming and quickly transferred to another ship and lay low in Cawsand Bay for a few hours while the *Bellerophon* left Plymouth Sound bound for Berry Head outside the approach to Torbay.

When Lord Keith took delivery of McKenrot's ultimatum on 5 August, the 'witness' was well out of reach and the Admiral had been spared the task of becoming Boney's keeper for four months before being dragged before the court.

A potentially embarrassing situation for the government had been avoided and, as Sir Walter Scott summarised the case in his *Life of Napoleon* (1827). reduced the risk of raising hopes amongst supporters of the determined asylum seeker:

Some newspaper, which was not possessed of a legal adviser to keep it right in form, had suggested (a tenderness, we suppose, to public curiosity) that the person of Napoleon Bonaparte should be removed to shore by an agency of a writ of Habeas Corpus. This magical rescript of the Old Bailey... loses its influence over an alien or prisoner of war and therefore, such an absurd proposal was not acted upon. But an individual, prosecuted for a libel upon a naval officer, conceived the idea of citing Napoleon as an evidence in a court of justice, to prove, as he pretended, the State of the French navy, which was necessary for his defence... Although this was a mere absurdity, and only worthy of the laughter with which the anecdote was generally received, yet it might have given rise to inconvenience, by suggesting to Napoleon, that he was, by some process or other, entitled to redress by the Common Law.

A writer styling himself 'Old Bailey', poured scorn on Capel Lofft's submission in an epic poem from which the following extract is taken:

Habeas Corpus

While the Law is so hard; and his brains are so soft,
Poor CAPEL, resolving to mount up aloft,
In The Chronicle prints a most learned opinion,
Upon Emperor BONEY; his crown and dominion;
For BONEY, alas! Being hunted about,
Like a rat in a jar, with no hole to get out,
For fear of the gallows, which BLUCHER long owed him,
To MAITLAND surrendered, who cruelly stowed him,
With the gang of his com-rogues, of rascals a score,
In the snug little hold of a seventy-four.

Well – down for the Brilliants the Barrister sits;
As completely as ever possessed of his wits,
The law to determine: - and what, pray, can fix it?
So well as the Barrister's own ipse dixit?
Magna Charta he copies, and learnedly cites
The Statue of CHARLES, and the famed Bill of Rights;
But oh! How he would in his reading have reckon'd
The Stat. de frangentibus, EDWARD the Second,
If CAPEL, and other such sapient law-seekers,
Such patriots, I mean, as have out of the dock ran;
Like Emperor NAPPY, and honest Lord COCHRANE.

And then for a prison! Sure never was seen a
More horrible dungeon than this Saint Helena!
So distant, so desolate, dreary, and dull!
No company there but a rat or a gull!

No Peers to create, and no conscripts to raise,
No Minions to please him, no Senates to praise!
Left alone without treasures, or armies, or ships,
'Tis odds if poor BONEY don't die of the hips!
The Counsellor, truly, is much disappointed.
His hopes discomposed, and his feelings disjointed,
To think that the glorious great Emperor NAP
Should be shut in a ship like a mouse in a trap,
Instead of enjoying his princely estate,
With plenty of money and jewels and plate,
To arrange his intrigues, and to make a fine show,
With LUCIEN and JOACHIM, JEROME and JOE;

With a Court of his Majesty's own special choosing –
Such modest requests who could think of refusing?
At least we should send him to Elba awhile,
That easy, convenient, snug sort of Isle,
From whence, any dark winter's night, without warning,
He may land with his soldiers in France before morning.

Ah, good Mister LOFFT! With one half of an eye,
A goose may your law and your loyalty spy!
Against St. Helena you make this resistance,
Because of its solitude, safety, and distance;
Where your idol, a wart on the face of the world,
May to hopeless oblivion be scornfully hurl'd.
Perhaps you're afraid, when no help's to be had,
The EMPEROR will with vexation go mad,
Till, finding himself from his gang kept apart,
He may break out of prison by breaking his heart.
He can make his escape, when of comfort bereft,
With a dose of the drug that from Jaffa* was left;

Or send of hot bullets a brace through his brain,
Or a razor apply to his jugular vein;
Or the halter, so much more becoming, and rob
Jack Ketch of the fee so long due for the job:
And really, the Felon on others should be
The same to himself, and turn Felo de se.

But don't be afraid! For the scoundrel, be sure,
Would rather all shame and all sorrow endure,
Than take up the poison, the rope, or the knife,
To do the least harm to his own precious life.
No, no – your fine hero would stand in the pillory,
And face rotten eggs and the cow-dung artillery,
Be pulled by the nose, and be kicked black and blue,
And run the vile gauntlet of infamy through,
One moment his worthless existence to save,
And escape from his worst of his terrors – the grave.

So make yourself easy, good Counsellor, pray,
For NAP to the Devil will scarce run away;
Though one time or other, you'll see by good hap,
That the Devil will run off with Emperor NAP
The sooner the better – so brush up your law,
Get the writ signed and sealed by old Lucifer's claw;
And e're to Helena we ship off the Porpuss,
Direct to the Devil your HABEAS CORPUS.
(*Morning Post*, Sat. 5 August 1815)

*During the seige of Jaffa, fought against the Ottoman Empire
in 1799, military doctors successfully opposed Napoleon's
suggestion that French soldiers afflicted by a plague epidemic,
should be poisoned

'Get the writ signed and sealed by old Lucifer's claw'

Angry and disappointed, Napoleon indicted a protest about the violation of his human rights, which he ordered to be sent to the British Ministry on 4 August, 1815:

> *I hereby solemnly protest, before God and man, against the injustice offered me, and the violation of my most sacred rights, in forcibly disposing of my person and liberty. I came freely on board the* Bellerophon; *I am not a prisoner, I am the guest of England. I was, indeed, instigated to come on board by the captain, who told me that he had been directed by his Government to receive me and my suite, and conduct me to England, if agreeable to my*

wishes. I presented myself in good faith, with the view of claiming the protection of the English laws. As soon as I had reached the Bellerophon, *I considered myself in the home and on the hearth of the British people. If it was the intention of the Government, in giving orders to the captain of the* Bellerophon, *to receive me and my suite merely to entrap me, it has forfeited its honour and sullied its flag.*

If this act be consummated, it will be useless for the English to talk to Europe of their integrity, their laws, and their liberty. British good faith will have been lost in the hospitality of the Bellerophon.

I appeal to history; it will say that an enemy, who made war for twenty years upon the English people, came voluntarily in his misfortune to seek an asylum under their laws. What more striking proof could he give of his esteem and his confidence? But what return did England make for so magnanimous an act? They pretended to hold out a friendly hand to this enemy; and when he delivered himself up in good faith, they sacrificed him.

It is conceivable that Napoleon expected the same level of sympathetic treatment afforded by Britain to another deposed ruler of his country, Louis XVIII. Between 1809 and 1814, the French monarch-in-waiting lived with his retinue at Hartwell House, near Aylesbury, the county town of Buckinghamshire. The sumptuous mansion, set in ninety acres of land, was let for a sum of £500 a year by the owner of the property, Sir Charles Lee. The impoverished king was forced to contribute towards the support of his family and household, therefore his once grand and imperious courtiers became agricultural workers, resorting to farming, raising chickens and keeping assorted livestock. Following Napoleon's first abdication and subsequent exile to Elba, Louis accepted an invitation to rule as King of France and signed the document in the library of Hartwell House on 20 April 1814. An editorial in *The News* was highly critical of, what was effectively a life sentence passed without trial upon Napoleon, and Louis VXIII's and Lord Liverpool's refusal to acknowledge public opinion in their 'persecution of fallen greatness' concluding that, 'If BONAPARTE were to throw his *cocked hat into France*, it would assemble a power, which LOUIS can never enjoy':

Let us no longer laugh at the cowardly and feeble measures of LOUIS. He has denounced NAPOLEON a rebel and traitor, and could only escape the chance of again opposing his better supported claims to the throne, or of encountering a fair trial of the man and his offences, by getting an English Administration to banish him, un-arraigned!... What will the French nation feel, on this subject; where the King dares not try the rebel he had denounced? Where he durst not even arrest him; but connived at an escape which he evidently wished, if not promoted? To what does all this tend, but to give base and solidity to the claims which could only be evaded by such disreputable means? We are acquainted with no one act committed during the course of our political lives, which reflects such disgrace upon the perpetrators of it, as this unmanly persecution of fallen greatness - a persecution which bespeaks terror, fear, jealousy, cowardice and cruelty so mixed and amalgamated, that you cannot tell which prevails. But our sage Governors fear public assemblages. They were never created by any brilliance of theirs; and they wisely thought that if 10,000 persons could scarcely be kept off boarding the Bellerophon, some leagues at sea, in cock-boats and punts, at the hazard of their lives, what proportion of curiosity and admiration might reasonably be expected on terra firma! If he had been announced to land, one half of England would have been on the spot in 24 hours! As for hanging him, according to the plan of The Times, the whole Grand Jury of England would have been present to find the Bill - they must have partitioned off Salisbury Plain for the Ladies, and sent for all the Allied Armies at Paris to keep the ground. The whole expense would have been readily defrayed by cutting up the gallows afterwards, into tooth-picks, and selling them at five and ten guineas a piece!

(*The News*, 13 July 1815)

The editor of *The News* also revealed details of a failed royal plan to cash in on the above mentioned 'curiosity and admiration expected on terra firma' by charging the public to view the celebrated warmonger Napoleon Bonaparte:

From the first moment that the person of Bonaparte has been in our power, the general talk but how much he was worth at a show! What a vast property

Exhibit in a cage: 'Bonaparte, all alive-o'!

might be realised by exhibiting in a cage at 5s [25p] per head! The Premier has been barricadoed with numerous propositions on this subject: and it has been said that a serious tender was made, offering to secure that sum annually to the Prince Regent's favourite brother, the Duke of Cumberland, which the House of Commons lately so parsimoniously refused; and also to furnish Carlton House and Windsor Cottage with various nick-knacks – such as golden Cupids, silver Venusses etc., provided full possession of the person of Napoleon was duly made over to the contractors. The Bard's fancy of 'tracing the noble spirit of an Alexander, till you found it stopping a bunghole' [Hamlet], were dignity itself compared to such a sixpenny show of Bonaparte, all alive-o!

(*The News*, 6 August 1815)

CHAPTER 5

Romantic Intrigue

Boney went a-courting
Way-aye-yah!
Leaving poor Josephine
Jean Francois!

Within hours of the arrival of the *Bellerophon* in Torbay, Lieutenant John Bowerbank observed Napoleon's reaction to the attention he was receiving from female admirers:

The English Fair Sex greet the invasion

Towards noon several thousand people were collected in hopes of getting a glimpse of our curiosity. He occasionally showed himself through the stern windows, and about three o'clock came upon deck viewing the crowd through his glass. He seemed struck with the beauty of the women, repeatedly crying out: 'What charming girls ! What beautiful women!' and bowing to them.

A Midshipman on the *Bellerophon*, George Home, recalled in a memoir how he was besieged by a large group of women questioning him about the celebrated passenger:

We came to an anchor in Torbay, when the first lieutenant was immediately put on shore, with orders to proceed by land to Plymouth, with dispatches for Lord Keith, at that time admiral on the Plymouth station. I happened to be midshipman of the boat which conveyed the first lieutenant on shore; and no sooner had we got clear of him than I was taken prisoner by some twenty young ladies, marched off to a fine house in the little town, regaled with tea and clouted cream, and bored with five thousand questions about Napoleon, the ridiculousness of which I have often laughed at since: What was he like? Was he really a man? Were his hands and clothes all over blood when he came on board? Was it true that he had killed three horses in riding from Waterloo to the Better option? Were we not all frightened of him? Was his voice like thunder? Could I possibly get them a sight of the monster, just that they might be able to say they had seen him? etc., etc. I assured those inquisitive nymphs that the reports they had heard were all nonsense; that the Emperor was not only a man, but a very handsome man, too; young withal; had no more blood upon his hands or clothes than was now upon their pure white dresses; that if by chance they got a look of him at the gangway they would fall in love with him directly; that, so far from his hands being red with blood, they were as small, white, and soft as their own charming fingers; and his voice, instead of resembling thunder, was as sweet and musical as their own. This account of the Emperor's beauty perfectly astonished the recluses of Torbay. Some misbelieved altogether,

'This account of the Emperor's beauty perfectly astonished the recluses of Torbay'

while the curiosity of others was excited beyond all bounds. A general proposition was now made that I should bundle them, like live cattle, into my little cutter, and take them all on board to gratify their curiosity at once. This was quite contrary to orders. Not a soul was allowed to come on board the ship, and I had to plead a thousand excuses for my want of gallantry in not complying with the very natural wish of my young companions. As far as I was concerned, resistance was vain. I was again seized, hurried down to the boat, and had the pleasure of seeing it filled to cramming with the charmers of Torbay. This was a devil of a mess. I might as well have gone into the mouth of a cannon as have carried such a cargo alongside the ship the thing was impossible. So I had nothing for it but to call aside the boat's crew and whisper to them to use gentle violence with my young boarders and set them down on shore. This was glorious fun to Jack. To work they fell, and in the midst of screams, laughter, and a few 'Damn my eyes, ma'am, don't kick so hard!' on the part of the Bellerophons, we had our nymphs safely deposited on terra firma and were off in a trice, enjoying the general discomfiture of the poor ladies, who were equally laughed at by the onlookers on shore.

In Torbay, Napoleon's attention was quickly drawn to a mysterious female on board one of the many small vessels that surrounded the *Bellerophon*. The romantic interlude was eloquently described by an eye witness and published in *Bailey's Magazine*:

The boats were rowing slowly round and round the Bellerophon, *with crews, it may be said, of devouring eyes. In one, from Torquay, was a lady wrapped, even in that warm weather, in a long mantilla. Her veil was closely drawn, and she evidently avoided observation. She was alone with a servant, and, notwithstanding the effort at concealment, her whole bearing betrayed a foreign origin. That rare elegance with which the shawl or mantilla is adjusted, and the grace that manipulated the light fluttering of a veil, belong to those who have made secrecy a law of social existence, and have converted an arrangement of colours into a language that more than speaks. She was a regal creature, moulded in that Giorgione form of voluptuousness, which embodies an epic of real and surpassing loveliness, and which, 'glowing and circumfused in speechless love', makes the entranced gazer, 'reeling in its fullness', turn away, 'dazzled and drunk with beauty'. By her side lay a choice bouquet. It was not an ordinary nosegay; the flowers had been cut short, tied on a stick or handle, and ranged in particular rows, and after a peculiar fashion –*

'By all the token flowers that tell
What words can never speak so well'.

The boat approached slowly, nearer and nearer, and then became stationary. The servant was despatched in another with the bouquet, and reached the accommodation ladder. Up it went with its special direction. The lady watched every movement with an eagerness and anxiety that stirred tremulously the mantilla and veil. You might almost fancy that you could hear the beating of her heart. The nosegay was passed onwards on the main deck, and reached the stage leading to the quarter deck. Then, in an agony of expectation, the lady lifted her veil, disclosing one of those glorious countenances that the sunny south produces, which 'now melt into sorrow, now madden to crime', those who are spellbound and possessed by the charms of this exceeding beauteousness.

Napoleon, at first, received and laid aside the bouquet without particular notice, but, looking at it again, he seized it suddenly, paused a moment, and then came hastily to the side of the ship. Shading his eyes with his hand, with a look of intensity that seemed to penetrate and transfix by its keen glance the object of regard, he caught at last in its range the bright vision he sought for. What a look of mingled emotion! The grey eye was fixed, full and fervidly, in an earnestness of devotion; one long, lingering gaze, soft and fond, yet, tinged with a passing shade, as if memory had performed for the moment an unwelcome duty. At that instant he was no longer a conqueror. Then came back the stern expression; and with the rapid fingers of his delicately-shaped hands he gave, precipitately, the signal message that was so hoped and longed for. Once more – a second, and in the next the boat was bounding over the blue water on its way back to Torquay. It was the last that the great Emperor ever saw of the beautiful Italian. Jealousy separated them; she was not permitted to accompany him to St Helena, and the mighty conqueror became obedient to the will of a worn-out harridan.

Napoleon's tangled romantic affairs were legion. During his failed Egyptian campaign, he took a young officer's wife as his mistress. He had a brief relationship with his brother Joseph's future sister-in-law and a longer one with Polish countess Marie Walewska. In 1796, he married Josephine de Beauharnais, the widow of a general guillotined during the 'terror' of the French Revolution. 'Citizen Beauharnais' herself, was only reprieved on the day set for her own execution. Ten years into the marriage, the adulterous Napoleon, acknowledged the existence of an illegitimate son, Charles, Count Leon. The child's mother was divorcee, Eleonore Denuelle. Although a mother of two from her first marriage, Josephine failed to provide Napoleon with the legitimate child he desired to found a dynasty.

Napoleon and Josephine's relationship appeared to be a genuine love-match, but at the age of forty, he cruelly told Josephine, 'I need a womb', then, summarily divorced her to marry eighteen-year-old Princess Marie Louise, the daughter of Francis, the first Emperor of Austria. The marriage formed part of the 1809 peace treaty between France and Austria. The union of Napoleon and Marie succeeded in providing an heir, Napoleon II, born in March 1811. From birth, the child was proclaimed the titular King

Empress Marie Louise

of Rome. Napoleon had the son he craved and announced, 'I trust he will fulfil his destiny'.

During Napoleon's sojourn in England, press reports emerged of a potentially life-threatening accident to the heir apparent that occurred near the imperial summer residence Schonbrunn Palace in Vienna:

A few days ago the young Napoleon, who still resides at Schonbrunn, was in great danger of losing his life in an airing to the village of St Viet, near Schonbrunn. Passing through the little river Wein, which was swelled a little, the force of the water, drove back the horses, by which the coach was overturned, and the young Prince, with the Lady, his attendant, fell into the water. One of the Emperor's footmen, who was with the carriage, immediately leapt into the water, and saved the Prince, who, however, with his usual liveliness, did not seem at all decomposed, and returned in high spirits to Schonbronn. Since his august mother has been absent, he often visits her in Baden, but always returns to Schonbrunn in the evening.

(*The News*, Sunday 30 July 1815)

Napoleon II was a babe in arms when his father retreated from Moscow in 1812 and only three at the time of Bonaparte's exile on Elba. When the elder Napoleon abdicated following his defeat at Waterloo, he nominated his four-year-old son to succeed him as Emperor of France. Whilst on board the *Bellerophon*, Napoleon was observed attempting to dispose of the draft of a letter on this subject by a sightseer who retrieved the torn fragments:

Napoleon II

Mr Mulligan, silk-mercer, of Bath, having repaired to Plymouth on Wednesday night, made the usual inquiries about the proper time to go out and see the great object of public curiosity: he was told five o'clock in the afternoon would be quite early enough; but impatient of delay, he secured a boat to himself, and proceeded about two o'clock towards the Bellerophon; *no other boat had at that time come out, and his was allowed to approach within fifty yards of the vessel, the guard-boat alone intervening. It was a short time after the final destination of Bonaparte had been officially communicated to him. Mr Mulligan soon observed Napoleon at the cabin window, in the act of* destroying papers, *which, after tearing into pieces, he* threw *into the sea. Mr Mulligan naturally anxious to secure some relics of this interesting character, picked up several fragments that drifted with the ebbing of the tide towards his boat; and on his return to Bath he discovered that they were of considerable interest, if not importance… the most perfect of the fragments is part of a letter from Bonaparte to Maria Louisa, evidently written immediately after his late abdication. It appears to have been the first copy, penned in Napoleon's hand, on paper made for his especial use, with his profile and signature,* (Napoleon, Empereur des Francois.) *in the water-mark. We subjoin a copy of the translation:-*

Madam, my dear and honoured Wife! Attending once more solely to the interests of France, I am going to abdicate the Throne; and in closing my own political career, to bring about the commencement of the reign of our dear Son. My tenderness for you and for him

Lord Keith boards 'Billy Ruffian'

impels me to this step no less than my duties as a Monarch. If he ensures, as Emperor, the happiness of France, and as a Son, the happiness and the glory of his Mother, my dearest wishes will be accomplished! Nevertheless, if even in his most tender infancy, I can give up to him all my authority, in my capacity of Head of the State, I cannot, and it would be too painful to my heart, to sacrifice also the inviolable rights which Nature gives me …

(*The Courier*, Saturday 12 August 1815)

Sadly, the young pretender never fulfilled his father's bold aims for his future. Losing his father at the age of ten, the sickly child endured years of ill-health before passing away, evidently from a bout of tuberculosis, at the age of twenty-one in July 1832. A traditional folk ballad, of uncertain origin, describes a scenario where the young Napoleon is in conversation with Marie Louise, assuring her that, during his brief life and impending death, his dream has been and still remains to avenge his father's memory and defeat the former Emperor's greatest foe, Great Britain, referred to in the title of the song as *The Bonnie Bunch of Roses*:

The Bonnie Bunch of Roses

By the margin of the ocean,
One pleasant evening in the month of June,
When all those feathered songsters
Their pleasant notes did sweetly tune,
'Twas there I spied a female
Who seemed to be in grief or woe,
Conversing with young Bonaparte
Concerning the Bonnie Bunch of Roses-O.

Then up spake young Napoleon
And took his mother by the hand,
Saying, 'Mother dear, be patient
Until I'm able to take command.
I'll build a mighty army
And through tremendous danger go.
And I never will return again
Till I've conquered the Bonnie Bunch of Roses-O.

'When first you saw great Bonaparte,
You knelt upon your bended knee
And asked your father's life of him

And he granted it most mournfully.
'Twas then he took his army
And o'er the frozen Alps did go;
Saying, 'I never will return again
Until I've conquered the Bonnie Bunch of Roses-O.

Napoleon leads his men over the Alps

'He took ten hundred thousand men
And kings likewise for to bear his train.
He was so well provided for
That he could sweep the world for gain.
But when he came to Moscow
He was overpowered by sleet and snow
And with Moscow all a-blazing,
He lost the Bonnie Bunch of Roses-O'.

'O, son, be not too venturesome,
For England has a heart of oak,
And England, Ireland, and Scotland,
Their unity has never been broke.
Remember your dear father;
In St Helena his body it lies low,
And if ever you follow after,
Beware of the Bonnie Bunch of Roses-O'.

'O mother, dearest mother,
Now I lie on my dying bed.
If I lived I might have been clever,
But now I rest my youthful head.
And when our bones lie mouldering
And weeping willows o'er us do grow,
The deeds of brave Napoleon
Shall conquer the Bonnie Bunch of Roses-O'.

CHAPTER 6
Dramatic Incidents

Boney contemplated suicide
Way-aye-yah!
Poison is the way to die
Jean Francois!

A memoir by the late John Smart of Brixham, was published in *Napoleon and his Fellow Passengers* (1908) recalling how he and some chums were thrown an exciting message in a bottle when they took out a small boat to the *Bellerophon* when the naval vessel first sailed past Berry Head into Torbay:

> *In common with most English schoolboys of that Waterloo year, we had an extra week's holiday at midsummer, and this was fortunate for me, as it*

Boney in hot water

tided me over my birthday on 24 July… As we rounded the bows of the ship the tide caught us with great force, and at the second time of our doing this, as luck would have it, we were taken a little nearer than we would willingly have ventured. As the current swept us along, I noticed at one of the lower-deck ports a man nodding violently to us, but standing back a little, as if frightened at being seen. His eye caught mine for an instant as he put his fingers to his lips with a warning gesture… as we passed he let something drop from his fingers into the water… It was a foreign-looking bottle, and as I drew the cork, its oiliness and perfume suggested that it had been used for some liqueur… In the bottle was a small piece of paper rolled up, and on the paper was written, 'We have got Bonaparte on board'.

In five minutes after we reached shore, there was not a soul in Brixham, except babies, ignorant of the news. Happy was the possessor of a boat on that day. Every sort of craft that could be pulled by oars or propelled by sail was brought into requisition. The people on board the ship must have suspected from the bustle on the quay that their secret was discovered; but the cries of 'Bonaparte! Bonaparte!' from all the boats, soon told them. Then, finding concealment useless, all the strange visitors showed themselves. We did not know who they all were for some days afterwards, and in fact only got a proper list from the London newspapers when the ships were gone. I can picture at this moment Boney as he appeared in the stern gallery of the Bellerophon. *My first thought was how little he looked, and that he was rather fat. We were not allowed to come near the ship, but we saw him quite plainly.*

He wore a green uniform with red facings, gold epaulettes, white waistcoat and breeches, and high military boots. He took off his hat, which had a cockade on it, and bowed to the people, who took off their hats and shouted 'Hooray!' I recall a feeling of triumph mixed with a natural satisfaction at seeing a wonderful sight. Bonaparte seemed to take all the excitement as a tribute to himself. We noticed that the English officers and crew were very respectful, and all took off their hats when they spoke to him.

Torquay was little else but a fisherman's village in those days, and was only beginning to be known by health-seeking visitors as a salubrious hamlet in Torre parish; but the population, such as it was, seemed to have turned out altogether and crossed the bay… The day was spent by us mostly on the water, and what an afternoon! The people of Dartmouth had already begun to come in, some on foot, some in carts and chaises, and others round Berry Head in boats. Boats! There never was before or since such an assembly of craft in Torbay as there was the next day. From Exmouth, Teignmouth, Plymouth, the boats and yachts continued to arrive all day. This was mainly on Tuesday, and on that day all the country seemed to come in. Gentlemen and ladies came on horseback and in carriages; other people in carts and waggons; and to judge by the number of people, all the world inland was flocking to see Bonaparte. The Brixham boatmen had a busy time of it, and must have taken more money in two days than in an ordinary month. It seemed a gala day as the boats thronged round the Bellerophon… *Brixham had already one glorious memory of a king when William of Orange touched English soil for the first time at Brixham Quay [in 1688]; and now we had the Emperor the conqueror, the tyrant, the villain a safe prisoner in an English ship.*

The enormity of the historic occasion and the clamour to catch a sight of Napoleon on the *Bellerophon* brought a warning about the dangers caused by vast numbers of jostling small craft. In a letter written from Exmouth on Tuesday 25 July 1815 and published in *The Times* three days later, the unidentified correspondent described the day's events in Torbay. Having taken out a pilot boat accompanied by a few friends who were 'gratified' to have seen Bonaparte repeatedly appearing for a period of two hours at his wide open cabin window, they 'anchored near the *Bellerophon* amidst thousands of boats', and were aware of a dangerous situation developing, 'It is impossible to describe the bustle we are in at Exmouth, every kind of vessel is put into requisition… and I fear some accidents will happen'.

The prophecy became grim reality in an incident that occurred on 31 July in Plymouth Sound. The tragic circumstances were reported in the press:

On Monday evening a boat, with two men, one woman, and three children, who were returning from visiting the Bellerophon *at Plymouth, was cut*

*'The Emperor, the conqueror, the tyrant, the villain a safe
prisoner in an English ship'*

into two pieces by a man of war's launch. The whole [party], however, were saved, with the exception of a stone-mason of his Majesty's dockyard, an industrious worthy man: husband of the [rescued] woman and father of the children. Two others who were picked up are not expected to live.

(*The News*, 6 August 1815)

A week later, as preparations for Napoleon's voyage into exile were underway, the event was marred by a further tragedy on the water resulting in the deaths of two members of the Harris family from Totnes:

We are sorry to state that the transferring of Napoleon Bonaparte from the Bellerophon *to the* Northumberland, *has been attended with a very serious accident, by which two ladies lost their lives. The letter which brings this information is from Torbay, and may be relied on. It is as follows:*

Torbay, Aug 8 – An accident happened last night off the Berry Head: a boat from Torquay, having on board three ladies, one gentleman, one child, one servant and two boatmen, went out to witness the transfer of Bonaparte from the Bellerophon *to the* Northumberland; *as she was sailing round the head of the latter vessel, she was met by a King's cutter, and before each were aware of the approach of the other, the boat was run down and instantly sunk. The first Lieutenant of the* Northumberland, *witnessing the distressing scene, leaped into the sea, and happily succeeded saving one of the ladies (Mrs Harris) and the child from a watery grave. Mr Harris, husband of the lady just mentioned, was saved by his own exertions, and by the exertions of the cutter's crew. The female servant and the two boatmen were also saved: but the other two ladies (both young), an aunt and niece, sunk to rise no more.*

(*The News*, 13 August 1815)

When the *Bellerophon* sailed along the English coast, one of the passengers on board the *Bellerophon*, Madame Fanny Bertrand, formerly a maid of honour to the Empress Josephine, burst into tears. She had spent much of her early life in this country, having been born on the island Martinique. Her English father, Count Dillon, served in the French army and became a victim of a terrible atrocity during the French Revolution when he was murdered. His dead body was horribly mutilated and then cannibalised by the royalist troops who mutinied under his command in 1792. On the *Bellerophon*, Madame Bertrand acted as a translator for Napoleon and read the daily newspapers to him. Lieutenant John Bowerbank observed the depressing effect that press reports had on the pair while reviewing the government's decision about their fate on 30 July:

> *It was on Sunday the papers announced the determination of sending Bonaparte to St Helena, and as he regularly enquires for them, perusing with the assistance of Madame Bertrand almost every item, that part did not long escape his notice... Before this I heard it was his determination never to quit the ship alive if to be sent to St Helena; and Madame Bertrand informed me the above, he had again positively asserted they should first take his life... On Monday, when he officially learned his destination, he*

French troops mutinied and killed Count Dillon

remained on deck but a short time, and appeared as pale as death... I fear, on the arrival of the Northumberland, *we shall witness some tragical scene.*

A circumstance occurred last Sunday night which appeared very near being a beginning to the scene I mentioned above. About nine o'clock Marshal and Madame Bertrand were walking on the opposite side of the deck to where I was, in earnest conversation, – suddenly Madame rushed into the Emperor's cabin, threw herself at his feet for about half a minute, then flying below to her own cabin, threw herself nearly out of the stern-window, when she was fortunately caught by the leg by General Montholon. The motive assigned I heard for this rash act was the determination of her husband to follow the fortunes of Napoleon whatever they might be, even to death. Madame Bertrand continued delirious the whole night. Under the apprehension that similar attempts might be made, boats were stationed round the ship until the morning...

Previous to our sailing [to rendezvous with HMS Northumberland *at Berry Head] Bertrand learned that the British Government had given its permission that he should accompany Napoleon. He seemed rejoiced at the*

Napoleon 'appeared as pale as death'

Fanny Bertrand was prevented from jumping into the sea

intelligence and the opportunity it afforded him of evincing his attachment. Madame Bertrand exerted all her influence, but in vain, to dissuade him from this exile. She is a gay, lively, high-spirited and dressy woman, and I think her eye and hopes were directed to a London residence in preference to one in St. Helena... We begin to suspect that she had no very sincere intention of self-destruction; but flattered herself that the 'scena' would perhaps have sufficient effect in mollifying her husband...

In consequence of orders from the Admiralty we sailed soon after twelve in company with the Tonnant, *Admiral Lord Keith, and the* Eurotas *frigate; and laid to in the offing for the* Northumberland. *All Napoleon's hopes sank with this movement. He now became very sullen; would not quit his cabin even for meals, but ate alone and rarely saw any person throughout the day. He still refused to name his future companions; declared his resolution never to be removed. We were all now in full expectation of some tragical event. The general conjecture was that he would end himself by poison. It was believed that he had in his possession a large quantity of laudanum. Madame Bertrand even hinted that ere morning we should find him a corpse... Madame Bertrand said to me: 'I promise you, you will never get the Emperor to St Helena; he is a man and what he says he will perform'... She afterwards declared to one of the ship's officers that 'she really believed the Emperor had now swallowed poison'.*

In Paris, three days after the Battle of Waterloo, Napoleon had swallowed a vial of poison he had carried during the campaign in case of capture. A pharmacist saved the leader's life by inducing prolonged vomiting by administering copious doses of emetic. However, contrary to speculation, the transfer from the *Bellerophon* to the *Northumberland* was completed without the anticipated 'tragical event'. Much to the surprise of the ship's officers, Napoleon's veiled threats of suicide proved to be without foundation as he demurely consented to undertake the seventy-day voyage into exile without further argument and meekly enquired about his destination: 'Is there any hunting or shooting there – Where am I to reside?' The manner of the prisoner's capitulation earned the disdain of John Bowerbank:

Napoleon attempted to take his own life after his defeat at Waterloo

This, indeed, is not the finale we expected. For although I am not prepared to say that he ever personally declared his intention of destroying himself, yet it has been an intention which his adherents have taken such pains to insinuate, that the persuasion of his doing so, in preference to being forced from the Bellerophon, *had taken full possession of our imaginations. It is difficult, however, to persuade oneself that they would ever have ventured to give currency to such a report without his connivance. It could only be done with a view of averting his impending doom; and on the bursting of the bubble the endeavour to attain this object by such means has not raised him in our opinion. Had he at the first (when refused a landing in England)*

'I cannot represent him to myself as a truly brave man'

submitted to the destiny to which he must have known the general voice of Europe had sentenced him, he would at least have obtained the credit of possessing a strength of mind superior to his fortune. In forming an estimate of his character, I cannot represent him to myself as a truly brave man.

CHAPTER 7
Bonaparte's Banishment

He went to Saint Helena,
Way-aye-yah!
There he was a prisoner,
Jean Francois!

Napoleon Bonaparte's brief sojourn in England came to an end after the British government concluded negotiations with her allies and carefully settled on St Helena as the former emperor's final destination. The remote island in the south Atlantic, situated 5000 miles from Europe, 1800 miles from South America, and 1200 miles from Africa, was the property of the East India Company. Therefore, as the island was neither

Boney in the Valley of the Shadow of Death

ruled by the British crown or under the jurisdiction of the English courts, this meant that the prisoner could be held indefinitely without trial.

Major-General Sir Henry Bunbury, Under Secretary of State for War and the Colonies, was the person appointed by the Cabinet to announce officially to Bonaparte that St Helena was the place of his future residence. The former emperor was also informed that he would be allowed to take four of his friends (plus their wives and children) and twelve domestics. As reprisals were being carried out against former aides of Napoleon in France, including Marshal Ney and Joachim Murat who had both been executed for treason, it was arranged that the remainder of his entourage would be transported to Malta. Bonaparte deliberated long and hard before announcing his travelling companions: General Bertrand and Madame Bertrand with their three children, Count and Countess Montholon and their baby son, Count Las Cases, General Gorgaud, nine men and three women servants. Napoleon was suffering from a bilious complaint, caused by the incident when he tried to poison himself in Paris, but his personal physician declined to accompany him to St Helena and a ship's doctor from the *Bellerophon*, Barry O'Meara, volunteered to go

Thrice married Albine de Montholon became Napoleon's lover on St Helena

in his place. Before sailing into exile, Napoleon fired a parting shot at Lord Liverpool's government about the decision to deny him asylum, stating that he would rather be imprisoned in England than have freedom of movement on St Helena:

I would rather die than go to St Helena, or be shut up in some fortress. I desire to live in the interior of England, a free man, protected by and subject to the law, and bound by any undertakings or measures that may be thought necessary; I do not wish to engage in any correspondence with France, nor interfere in any political matters. … The idea of being sent to St Helena is a perfect horror to me. To be placed for life on an island in the Tropics, at an immense distance from any land … it is worse than Tamerlane's iron cage. … Had they confined me in the Tower of London or one of the fortresses in England (though not what I had hoped from the generosity of the English people) I should not have so much cause of complaint; but to banish me to an island within the Tropics! They might as well have signed my death warrant at once.

The government's position on how Napoleon was to be treated on St Helena was explained at a ministerial briefing published in *The Courier,* Friday 11 August:

As a great deal of misapprehension appears to exist on the subject of St Helena as a proper place for the confinement of BONAPARTE, we cannot avoid observing that the sentiments of many of our correspondents are founded upon the supposition: First, that BONAPARTE is to be at liberty on that island. Secondly, that neutral vessels are to have access to it. Thirdly, that the garrison is not to be trusted, and that the island does not belong to the Crown, but to the East India Company.

With respect to the first objection, we can assure our readers that there is no intention of suffering BONAPARTE to be at liberty in the island: he will be as regularly guarded and confined as he could be in England, and permitted only to take air and exercise when properly attended.

In the second place, all neutrals whatever will be excluded from the island as long as BONAPARTE is to continue a prisoner there; so that no danger on this account can possibly exist.

In the third place, he will be placed under the custody of a General Officer in the King's service, and of a British Admiral; the former will have the government of the island under the present circumstances. The garrison of the East India Company will be reduced or wholly withdrawn, and the island will be garrisoned by a King's regiment.

An officer of the East India Company, who had served on the island, provided a bleak, poetical picture of what would prove to be Napoleon Bonaparte's final destination:

Description of the Island St Helena

Rugged rocks and lofty mountains,
Interspers'd with crystal fountains,
Here and there a grove of trees,
Are all the wandering stranger sees:
The tradesmen, imitating fops,
With heads as empty as their shops;
The girls, dressed out from head to toe,
Like painted dolls in puppet-show;
Unsocial wretches here reside,
Alike their poverty and pride,
Throughout this Isle, there's scarce a creature
With either breeding, or good nature;
For rugged rocks, and barren fields,
*Are all that St Helena yields.**

*Except an abundance of water-cresses and plenty of fish.
(*The News*, Sunday 20 August 1815)

Predictably, in view of the sympathetic stance that the newspaper had adopted over Napoleon's plight, an editorial in *The News*, published on Sunday 6 August, was highly critical of the government's handling of the issue:

Cruelty and persecution will now only canonize BONAPARTE. It will speak more than a thousand victories, the fearful ascendancy of the man's mind over the legitimate Princes of our days. They may hem him round by rocks and oceans, and station an army to watch him. This is but a humiliating confessional on their parts. In the meantime, the calm conduct

of the captive, the preserved tranquillity of his mind, amid reverses without parallel, in their extremity, excite as much the astonishment of the philosopher, as the conquests have formerly astounded all military foresight and calculation… Had the Executive Government adopted the blustering and brutal feelings of The Times, *and have brought* NAPOLEON *to a sham trial, on sham charges, and condemned him to be hanged, there were*

Napoleon with his male companions on St Helena

a decision and courage in their policy which would have snatched it from utter and irretrievable contempt. We might have honoured such a conduct with our simple and unmixed abhorrence. But to smother a man's life, which has been thrown on our mercy, in the living tomb of banishment on a foreign land, were a deed fit only for a Romance made up of the very disease of horrors.

Napoleon reflects on his downfall at Longwood on St Helena

Napoleon Bonaparte survived on St Helena for less than six years. Diagnosed with stomach cancer at the age of fifty-one, he died at a rundown villa, Longwood House, on 5 May 1821. The following day, an officer serving on St Helena, wrote a letter, noting that the death had ironically occurred three days after the merchant vessel *Waterloo* had anchored at St Helena:

I have just returned from witnessing an awful spectacle – the body of the deceased General Bonaparte, late the terror of whole Europe... I may say that I had the earliest opportunity of seeing him, and of being in his company, of any person on the island, and nearly the last view and touch of his body. I lived under the same roof for seven weeks on his first arrival, and had an opportunity of a great deal of conversation with him; during which time he was very pleasant and agreeable with the family I resided with [where Napoleon was also accommodated until renovations were carried out on Longwood]: since which I have seldom seen him until today, when he was lying in the full dress of a General of the Legion of Honour, and appeared to be more like a person asleep than a corpse, and very little altered from when I saw him. On his countenance there was the appearance of a pleasant smile. He is to be interred on a spot chosen by himself some time previous to his death. It is under a willow tree (about ten yards from a spring of water, from which he has been supplied ever since his residence at Longwood), in a valley called by the natives the 'Devil's Punchbowl' [henceforth known as Napoleon's Vale].

(*The Times* 11 July 1821)

The carpenter, tasked with furnishing a coffin for the occasion, wrote a letter home describing his part in the demise of Napoleon:

I received orders for the coffins for the illustrious deceased, which were of course executed with all possible dispatch. Enclosed with him in the coffin was a silver urn containing his heart, and another containing his stomach, and all the coins that were issued during his reign; together with a knife and fork, a spoon, one plate, all of silver. The pall at the funeral was of purple velvet… and on the head of the coffin a cushion and crucifix.

(*Trewman's Exeter Flying Post*, 9 August 1821)

The auspicious funeral of Napoleon was described in a letter from a naval officer 'high in command' on St Helena:

He was buried with the highest military honours and every person in full dress. We had to go full two miles: and the procession, and two thousand troops followed after the procession had passed with their arms reversed, was a remarkably fine sight. We of the procession were mounted on horseback until he began to descend the hill, and the body was placed on a car drawn by his own horses. His riding horse was led after it, dressed in the style he rode when at the head of his armies. The sword and mantle he wore when at the Battle of Marengo were displayed on the coffin.

(*The Times*, 11 July 1821)

The highlights of Napoleon Bonaparte's rise to power and his decline to ignominious death was summarised at the time in the following verses by poet Hafiz:

The Death of Napoleon

On the Death of Napoleon

Though fortune raised Napoleon to a throne,
From an estate comparatively low,
'Twas not enough – the world his sway must own!
Thus his ambition proved his overthrow.

Yet his success seemed equal for a time,
To the vast projects that his genius planned
His martial prowess and career sublime,
Europe appeared unable to withstand.

At length the North to his rapacious course,
An unexpected barrier opposed –
Russia repelled the bold Invader's force,
And Waterloo his baffled efforts closed.

Then sank the splendour of that blazing star,
The terror of the troubled world before;
Chained to a rock, secure, and distant far,
The Imperial Eagle soared aloft no more,

And now the final doom, that in their turn
Shall all the race of mortal man betide,
Consigns the far-famed Hero to his urn –
The hapless victim of unbounded pride.
(*Morning Post*, 13 July 1821)

Napoleon's remains were exhumed and transported to Paris in 1840

Echoing Lieutenant John Bowerbank's thoughts on the *Bellerophon*, that Napoleon's disgrace was a worse fate than death, the following magazine article argued that it would have been preferable to have died a soldier's death:

Napoleon should have died at Waterloo. He has been from that hour worse than dead... Napoleon is now beyond the power of disturbing the world... He was a tyrant in the darkest sense of the name... He was felt to be that enemy of mankind whom no faith could bind – to have suffered him on a throne would have been only to prepare new misfortune for the earth. He was declared an outlaw by the hearts of all nations, before he was by their lips; and after having run the career of a villain, he died the death of a slave – stripped of empire, fame and public commiseration, from a hopeless dungeon to a dishonoured grave.

(Blackwood's Edinburgh Magazine, August 1821)

CHAPTER 8
Napoleonana Bonaparteana

Boney was a warrior
Way-aye-yah!
A warrior and a terrier
Jean Francois!

Some contemporary newspapers covering The Battle of Waterloo and its aftermath included a round-up of press comment, poems, anecdotes,

The Grande Finale played by the Crown Heads of Europe

bizarre stories and intriguing facts surrounding Napoleon's plight and subsequent treatment in regular columns headlined 'Napoleonana' or 'Bonaparteana':

La Belle Alliance

On 6 July 1815, the Covent Garden Theatre presented *La Belle Alliance* (the name of an inn at the centre of Napoleon's line at the Battle of Waterloo) which featured the following musical tribute composed by James Kenney and M.P. King:

The Battle of Waterloo

On the green heights of Waterloo,
The Briton waits the day;
His arm is strong, his heart is true,
For dire must be the fray;
Europa, wilt thou yet be free,
It is a day of doom to thee.

Advances of the destroying host,
The battle rushes on,
Thy glory claims thy utmost boast,
Immortal WELLINGTON!
Such wreath awaits the victor now,
As never deck'd a victor's brow.

Thine is the God-like Hero's part
Assail'd in fury's form,
Thine eagle eye, thy lion heart
Still rule the bloody storm:
From early noon to set o'sun
The fight is neither lost nor won.

Hark! 'tis the Tyrant's curse is heard,
His rage is spent and gone;
Charge home! Is now thy battle word
Triumphant WELLINGTON!
To Britain, glory, freedom true,
Thine is the day of Waterloo!
(*Morning Post*, 5 July 1815)

La Belle Alliance inn near Waterloo

Boney is snuffed out!

Napoleon's Surrender Disbelieved in France

We are informed by a gentleman who has left Paris within these last few days that the account of Bonaparte's surrender to this country, and his subsequent removal to St Helena, are wholly disbelieved in France by the great mass of the population. They laugh at the thing as a ridiculous story invented by the partisans of Louis XVIII, to strengthen their own cause, and weaken the Bonapartists. The general belief is that Bonaparte is still in France, and he will soon reappear at the head of an army to dispute once more the sceptre with Louis. Such are the consequences of a shackled press. It is known that nothing can be admitted into the Paris Papers but what the government permits, and hence truth and falsehood are received with equal incredulity.

(*The News*, 20 August 1815)

King Bee Bonaparte

Napoleon chose the bee as his personal emblem as he admired the industriousness of the insect. For his coronation on Sunday 2 December 1804, 365 gold embroidered bees, representing each day of the year, were stitched on to his robes:

NAPOLEON BONAPARTE, in adopting the BEE, as his emblem, did not refer, by a moral feeling, to industry; but by a political *one to that extraordinary* instinct *which develops an order and a power, in the communities of that insect, superior to the results of reason among mankind. What constitutes the power of association in the Bee? The control of an individual, on whose movements the fate and fortune of the whole hive attend. A point to* swarm *upon.*

Were Ministers afraid *of landing that extraordinary man on our shores, lest* this *country should* swarm *on him too? Does he bear a talisman which disarms enmity and conciliates esteem and friendship wherever he goes? Look at the descent of NAPOLEON from the coast of Elba. The order, alertness, unresisting and undividing union with which France formed upon his movement, gave a beautiful illustration to the emblem of their extraordinary leader. He is a kind of* King *Bee, of principles and feelings in France, which are indestructible: the submission of the army discloses to us this fact… Was a nation ever beaten out of its opinions?… France never loved BONAPARTE more than in his adversity. His army never fought so desperately valorous as in the fatal battle of Waterloo.*

(*The News*, 20 August 1815)

The Charge of the Scots Greys at Waterloo

A man of the Scots Greys, from Ayrshire, has eighteen sword and sabre wounds, the greater number of which were inflicted by those savages after he was on the ground, dismounted. His name is Laurie, and a few days previous to the battle he had accounts of his father's death, by which this gallant private soldier became possessed of £12,000. He says that he saved his life in the end by calling out in French, as the enemy were charging over him, 'Oh! Mon Dieu! Mon Dieu! Mes amis! Mes amis!'– by which contrivance he was taken for one of their own men.

(*The News*, 6 August 1815)

Wounded Prisoners Arrive at Plymouth

While on the deck of the *Bellerophon* on Friday 28 July, Lieutenant John Bowerbank observed a poignant scene in Plymouth Sound:

This day several transports passed very near the Bellerophon, *bringing over the French prisoners taken in the battle of Waterloo, many of whom were wounded. Several of these poor fellows with their bandages, etc., were on deck. I am unable to speak as to the effect this sight (if he were witness of it)* may have had upon Bonaparte, as he was at the time in his cabin. His officers beheld them pass from the poop, the ideas with which it must have been associated could not but render it an affecting scene, and to do them justice they appeared to feel it.*

*Press reports noted that 'Bonaparte earnestly looked upon the prisoners from the stern gallery of the Bellerophon, *during the time they were passing that ship'.*

(*The News*, 6 August 1815)

The Battle of Mont St Jean

A private letter from Mons dated 14 July 1815, described the aftermath of the Battle of Waterloo (known as the Battle of Mont St Jean in France):

It is only within these four days that the business of interring the bodies which strewed the field of battle of Mont St Jean was finished. Several thousands of carriages had been put in requisition in the department of Jemappes for this operation. At the end of ten, twelve, and fifteen days, there were found among the dead a great number of wounded, who, from hunger or madness, had torn with their teeth the carcasses of men and horses. When I say from madness, *I use that term because there were actually men wounded and dying, who when they were picked up cried, 'Vive L'Empereur! Long live the man who brought us hither to be slaughtered, who left us behind in his flight, without caring whether we were dead or dying! Long live the man without pity, without feeling, who left us to expire slowly on the field of battle, without recommending us to the attention or humanity of any one, while the wounded of the other armies were collected with such care and anxiety'.*

(*The News*, 30 July 1815)

Duel Between Blucher and Bonaparte

Last week, at South Shields, two old Sons of Neptune differed in political opinions over a cask of grog. One of the heroes (who had a wooden leg) maintained that Bonaparte was a greater General than Blucher, which so enraged his opponent, that he dared him to the field of honour to decide the quarrel, where it was agreed that each was to assume the character of his favourite General.

Before the personifier of Blucher marched out, he caused epaulettes to be painted on the shoulder of his shirt with blood, thrust his head into a flour sack in order to resemble the veteran's hoary locks, and blackened his face with burnt cork in imitation of moustaches. Each armed with a firelock, attended by a number of followers, went to a neighbouring field, where, at no great distance, they levelled their pieces at each other and fired. Blucher's wadding struck poor Bonaparte, who, supposing himself shot by a bullet, gave a horrid yell, and fell down. Some of the spectators who were in on the secret, informed him that the gun was only loaded with blank cartridge, but advised him to pretend he was mortally wounded; and to do him justice, he imitated the dying scene to admiration. The news that Bonaparte was dead soon reached Blucher, who wept bitterly for the supposed horrid murder. His friends, at length, relieved him from his anxiety, when all animosity was drowned in hearty draughts of grog.

(*Royal Cornwall Gazette*, 19 August 1815)

Momentos, Souvenirs and Money Making Schemes

Waterloo provided a rich harvest of death and the unedifying spectacle of soldiers looting the bodies of friend and foe, vying with local peasants who surged onto the battlefield plundering and stripping corpses. The most valuable commodity was teeth collected by hammer and chisel from the mouths of the dead. Set in hippopotamus ivory, they provided dentures for the wealthy in a trade henceforth known as 'Waterloo teeth'. Ironically, late in life, the Duke of Wellington acquired a set for his own use, although the battle of origin was not disclosed.

Napoleonana stimulated a range of souvenirs and boatmen's money-making schemes:

Wellington Knockers!

Among other things bearing the glorious name are knockers to doors. At the top is a hand grasping a Marshal's staff, from which hangs a wreath of laurel: the head of a British lion at the foot of the wreath beats, when the knocked is used, a French eagle!

(*Trewman's Exeter Flying Post*, 14 December 1815)

Wellington Boot

The Boatmen Saw Him Coming

Impelled by a curiosity which has lately carried to Plymouth, the inhabitants of many parts of Great Britain, a particular friend of mine, Mr Timmins, set out from his seat in Lancashire and travelled night and day till he reached the important spot – leaped at once from his chaise into a boat, and immediately made towards the Bellerophon. *And now indeed, he was amply compensated for the fatigue and expenses of his journey. More fortunate than most others who have been on the same expedition,* he was *allowed to advance to within about a league and a half from the ship, and, then, with the aid of a bad telescope, which his boatman kindly lent him, for only an additional five shillings (25p), he saw, (as the said boatman told him) the 'vanquished victor' walking the quarter deck!! He indeed had the good fortune to be so* near *(having bribed one of the guard-boats with a pound note) that had he been a* little *nearer, he* might *also have seen Bonaparte take a pinch of snuff, for so his boatman assured him: even as it was he could discern that Bonaparte was a lot taller than we, who have not been to Plymouth, supposed him; and is so well satisfied as to the colour of his coat [widely reported to be green] that he offered to bet me a thousand pounds to a guinea, it was either dark blue or scarlet.*

(Letter from J.P. *Royal Cornwall Gazette*, 2 September 1815)

A Visit to Bonaparte in Plymouth Sound
By a Lady, Plymouth, 1815

There is nothing; so dull as mere fact, you'll admit,
While you read my detail, unenlivened by wit,
My friends will believe, though they're told it in rhyme
That I thought to return in a far shorter time.
When at once we're resolv'd, by half past on the move,
And by two, but a trio, we reach Mutton Cove;
When approaching the quay, such a rabble and rout,
That we ask 'My good friend, what is all this about?'
'They are rowing a race, and some boats are come in,
While these people are waiting till t'others begin'.

Well aware of our folly, with risible lip,
The boatman we told to make haste to the ship;
On the colours of fish, here by hampers full landing,
We gaze for amusement, while still we're kept standing;
At length to the Admiral's stairs we have got,
See his party on board, and bear tunes from his yacht.
The day is delightful, the gale just enough
For the sea to look lively without being rough.
With those first at the ship, our sight costs the dearer,
As we've longer to wait, and not, in the end, nearer;
For by land, and by water, so different the case is,
'Twas long before we were jam'd into our places;
But on further advice we'll at present be dumb,
For half the spectators you know, are now come:
In one boat, a bevy, all sarcenet and veil,
In the next some good fellows while toping their ale.
'Avast! Here's the guard boat. Aye here it comes smack'.
And the ladies cry 'Captain they'll drive us all back'.
Then some bully our men, with 'Scull out there, scull out',
And others check these with 'Mind what you're about'.
Here's a crazy old boat, laded dry by a shoe,
There, a gay painted barge is forced on our view;
In this, while Don Solus is jeered by the mob,
'See that empty boat, turn it out. Here's a fine job'.
Cries one, of some dozens squeezed into the next,
'I've left the pork, Oh dear I'm so vex'd'.
In the long boat, that shows us profusion of oar,
From the Captain bursts forth, a most terrible roar
At his men, but the anger about who, or what,
Though they still remember, we soon had forgot.
Here infants were crying, mothers scolding downright,
While the next party laughs at some comical sight.
Now watches and spy-glasses make their appearance,
And Impatience, that vixen, begins interference;

To beguile her, through portholes we eagerly stare,
For the nobles on deck are all taking the air.
'Hey dey what a bustle!' then 'All safe, all safe'.
The crowd is return'd to its chatter and laugh.
'Pray what was the matter?' From that boat, near the ship,
A woman fell over, and so got a dip'.
But a hum of applause, yes, his triumph is full,
Yet this hum of applause has betrayed our John Bull,
'What hum of applause? come I prithee be brief':
Why John was delighted to see them ship beef.
With a smile 'tis observed by the Briton polite,
How the glee of the crowd was improved, by the sight.
For the rough, honest tar, had declared from his heart,
That he thought this a sight that would beat Bonaparte.
Some, again, with composure, predict peace and war,
Others look at the great folks, and fancy a star;
But we, much fatigued, six o'clock now approaching.
And on our good nature we thought them encroaching.
When boats are made bridges, nay, tempted to think.
That through some of these freedoms, not strange we should sink.
But here I must mention, when all was most merry.
As here is each size, from the long boat to wherry.
When the crowd should disperse, I was fearful, I own,
Lest your small boats, by barges, should then be run down.
But a truce with our hopes, our predictions and fears,
For now, yes at last, our grand object appears;
And now every eye to the ship is directed,
Though to see Bonaparte, I no longer expected;
For between us what number of men! And aghast
We stood, as still thicker and thicker the mass.
But now see Napoleon, who seems in his figure,
What we call mediocre, nor smaller, nor bigger;
For in spite of our fears, how it was, I can't tell,
What our distance allowed of, we saw very well.

But in this we're full right, for now, hurry scurry,
Boat rows against boat, with the madness of fury;
The show was all over, but time was outstayed
By some, and by others, attempts were still made
To get round the ship, in hopes Bonaparte might
At some place yet be seen, thus to perfect their sight
(Reproduced in *English Caricature and Satire on Napoleon I*, 1888)

Tales of Redundant Sailors

With the Napoleonic Wars finally at an end, the British government announced stringent cuts to be made to naval ships and personnel. The following round up of press snippets gave details of the reduced strength of the navy; the perceived threat to public order from redundant sailors; an example of how some enterprising beggars posing as former sailors were earning a lucrative income; the shocking revelation that a young lady who had passed herself off as a seaman had married one of her former shipmates after being banished from the service:

Orders have been given to reduce the Navy of Great Britain to 12,000 Seamen, and 5,000 Marines. Twelve sail of the line are to be kept in commission for guard-ships, and one ship of the line for the East India station. All ships bearing flags on foreign stations are to be of the rank of 50 guns. ... Two hundred sail of men of war are under orders to be paid off.
(*The News*, 30 July 1815)

One of the Ministerial Papers, The Morning Herald *of Thursday last, stopped the press at two o'clock in the morning to inform its readers that a dark coloured carriage, with four horses, and attended by an escort of Dragoons, had just passed through the Strand, in the direction of the Tower [of London]. The inference to be drawn from this wonderful intelligence was obvious - Bonaparte was in the carriage ... but the fact is there was no such carriage passed through the Strand at that time, and therefore all comment on such a circumstance falls to the ground. On Thursday an additional guard of 100 men were marched into the Tower. This was at the moment deemed a confirmation of the silly report in* The Herald, *but on inquiry we learnt that from the representation of the Civil Magistrates, more soldiers are considered necessary in that part of the town; the numerous bodies of sailors now out of employ very naturally give rise to some apprehensions.*

(*The News*, 6 August 1815)

The Strand, from Somerset House to Charing Cross, if well begged, *is considered the most productive district in Westminster. It is now taken possession of by a number of fellows, pretending to be lame sailors, who on an average make twenty shillings a day (£1) each, and beat off all mendicant obtruders.*

(*The News*, 30 July 1815)

A short time since, one of the apprentices on board the Cicero *transport, then lying in Lisbon, was discovered to be female, of about 17 years of age, who had left her friends at Brighton, about four months earlier, and during which time she had undergone every fatigue and duty common to sea-apprentices. After the circumstances became known, she proved to be in love with one of the seamen; and on Saturday they were married in Portsmouth. The name of the adventurous fair one was Sarah Oram – the man, James Scott.*

(*The News*, 30 July 1815)

The Allies and Bonaparte

The instability of human grandeur affords food for reflection to the contemplative mind. A few, very few years, make a wonderful revolution in human affairs, and consequentially, in human affections – the mutability of political attachments is proverbial – hence the reverses of the ex-Emperor of France are very easily accounted for. On the 25 June 1807, the Emperor of Russia and France (Bonaparte) embraced each other on a raft in the Niemen. On the following day, the King of Prussia joined the two Sovereigns, and made a trio, giving the Emperor Napoleon the fraternal hug! In the month of July 1815, this same Emperor Napoleon is compelled

French and British troops clash during the Napoleonic Wars

by the Sovereigns who fraternised with him on board the raft, to run from the Throne of France and to fly to England for succour; and the Government of England send him, not on board a raft, but a man of war, to a private station in the Island of St Helena. Sic transit Gloria mundi! [Thus passes the glory of the world].

An old Grecian [nickname for inhabitants of Exeter] says, the only effect

of the late war will be, to transfer Napoleon from Paris to Helen. But the Helen of Ancient Greece was the cause of a long ten years' war – we hope the present Helen will be a means of securing to the world a lasting peace.
(*Trewman's Exeter Flying Post*, 10 August 1815)

Bonaparte's Conversation

On 7 August 1815, William Lyttleton MP, boarded the *Northumberland* with his friend Rear Admiral Sir George Cockburn who was the senior naval officer charged with conveying Napoleon to St Helena. In 1810, Lyttleton had gained notoriety for opposing the voting of an annuity to Wellington, whose merits he 'considered to be far short of those of Nelson'. During a conversation with Napoleon, Lyttleton conducted what, in essence, was the only interview given during the former emperor's sojourn in England:

Bonaparte: taking a pinch of snuff, broke out into some invectives against the conduct of the Allies; called it 'perfidious, treacherous'.

Lyttleton: But you seem to forget that you were in Elba in virtue of a solemn treaty – that no molestation was offered you, yet you left it in violation of the faith of that treaty?

Bonaparte: 'I was an independent Sovereign – I had a right to make war upon another Sovereign - upon Louis XVIII, if I chose'.

Lyttleton: Why are you surprised and indignant that you are to be sent to St Helena?

Bonaparte: I would have given my word of honour to have remained quiet, and to have held no political correspondence in England. I would have pledged myself to quit the place assigned me, but to live as a simple individual'.

Lyttleton: That seems to be next to impossible, for though you have had great reverses, you could never so far forget what you had been as to conceive yourself to be, or conduct yourself as a private individual?

Bonaparte: But why not let me remain in England upon my parole of honour?

Lyttleton: What are your feelings toward the Prince Regent?

Bonaparte: He is the only Sovereign in Europe that has been consistent, constant and vigorous – it is he who has been the real cause of defeating all my designs and destroying my career.

(*The News*, 20 August 1815)

Voyage to St Helena

A letter from Portsmouth Bay: 'Abundance of groceries, and all kinds of sea stock, were shipped with the utmost expedition on board the Northumberland, *for Bonaparte. Some hundreds of sheep, and several hundred tons of hay, were shipped to stock St Helena (where they remain) at the end of the voyage. Nothing seemed spared fit for an Ex-Emperor'… His cabin in the* Northumberland *is fitted up with great elegance. His bed is peculiarly handsome, and the linen upon it very fine. His toilet is of silver: among other articles upon it is a magnificent snuff-box, upon which is embossed in gold an eagle with a crown, flying from Elba to the coast of France – the eagle just seeing the coast of France, and the respective distances are admirably executed… His baggage consisted of two services of plate, some articles in gold, and a superb toilet of plate, beds, books etc., which he took with him… Napoleon's field library carried during his last campaign consisted of the following works: The Bible, Homer, Manon Lescant, Bossuet, La Pucelle, The History of Henry IV, The Conspiracy of Rienzi, La Pitte (poem by Delille), The Anarchy of Poland, La Fontaine's Tales, History of the Progress and Downfall of the Roman Republic, Don Quixote, Treaties of Peace by Martens, Gil Blas, Memorial of the Revolution, The Devil Upon Two Sticks, The Revolution of Corsica, The Amusements of Spa… Sir George Cockburn asked him if he wanted anything more before they put to sea. Bertrand replied, twenty packs of cards, a backgammon and domino table, and Madame Bertrand desired to have some necessary articles of furniture, which, it was said, should be furnished forthwith.*

(The News, 13 August 1815)

Inflation on St Helena

Further particulars of Bonaparte's arrival have reached us in letters from that island… The inhabitants naturally were struck with no small degree of surprise. It was of course learned at the same time, that a very considerable addition would be made to the population of the island by the new garrison, as well as the attendants of the celebrated Rebel, the commissioners to watch him, their suites, etc. Accordingly all was immediately hustle and bustle. Provisions experienced a sudden and enormous increase in price. Eggs, which were before three shillings a dozen, now advanced to a shilling each. Almost every other article of produce rose in the same proportion, and even land itself assumed an increased value of 50%, which is not much to be wondered at considering the small extent of the island, and the still smaller portion that is fit for cultivation.

(Trewman's Exeter Flying Post, 14 December 1815)

Hoax at Chester

A short time ago, a respectable looking man caused a number of handbills to be distributed through Chester, in which he informed the public that a great number of genteel families had embarked at Plymouth, and would certainly proceed with the British regiment appointed to accompany Bonaparte to St Helena: he added further, that the island being dreadfully infested with rats, his Majesty's Ministers had determined that it should forthwith be effectually cleared of those noxious animals. To facilitate this important purpose he had been deputed to purchase as many cats and thriving kittens as could possibly be procured for money in a short space of time; and, therefore, he publicly offered, in his handbills, 16 shillings [80p] for every athletic full grown tom cat, 10 shillings [50p] for every adult female puss, and half-a-crown [25p] for every thriving vigorous kitten, that could swill milk, pursue a ball of thread, or fasten its fangs in a dying mouse. On the evening of the third day after this advertisement had been distributed, the people of Chester were astonished with an eruption of a multitude of old women, boys and girls, into their streets, every one of whom carried on their shoulders either a bag or a sack, which appeared pregnant with some restless animal, that seemed labouring into birth. Every road – every lane was thronged with this comical procession – and the wondering spectators of the scene were involuntarily compelled to remember the old riddle about St Ives:

As I was going to St Ives,
I met fifty old wives,
Every wife had fifty sacks,
Every sack had fifty cats,
Every cat had fifty kittens,
Kittens, cats, sacks and wives,
How many were going to St Ives?

Before the night a congregation of nearly 3,000 cats was collected in Chester. The happy bearers of these sweet voiced creatures proceeded all (as directed by the advertisement) towards one street with their delectable burdens. Here they became closely wedged together. A vocal concert soon ensued. The women screamed – the cats squalled – the boys and girls shrieked treble, and the dogs of the street howled bass, so it soon became difficult to the nicest ear to ascertain whether the canine – the feline – or the human tones were predominant.

Some of the cat-bearing ladies, whose dispositions were not of the most placid nature, finding themselves annoyed by their neighbours, soon cast down their burdens, and began to box. A battle royal ensued. The cats sounded the war-whoop with might and main. Meanwhile, the boys of the town, who seemed to mightily relish the sport, were actively employed in opening the mouths of the deserted sacks, and liberating the cats from their forlorn situation. The enraged animals immediately bounded on the shoulders and heads of the combatants, and ran spitting, squalling and clawing along the undulating sea of skulls, towards the walls of the houses *of the good people of Chester. The citizens attracted by the noise, had opened the windows to gaze at the fun. Into these windows the cats instantly sprung, taking possession of the rooms by a kind of storm or escalade. The cats in their sudden assault on the drawing rooms and other apartments of the Chesterites, rushed with the rapidity of lightning up the pillars, and then across the balustrades and galleries, for which the town is so famous, and so slap-dash through the open windows into the apartments. Never since the days of the celebrated Hugh Lupus [Norman Earl of Chester, who fathered several illegitimate children] were the drawing rooms of Chester filled with a crowd of unwelcome guests. Now were heard the crashes of broken china – the howling of affrighted lap dogs – the cries of distressed damsels, who wept their torn faces and dishevelled charms – and the groans of fat old citizens, rushing and tumbling forward before the balconies, with heads divested of wigs – bald, bare, and bleeding. All Chester was soon in arms – and dire were the deeds of vengeance executed on the feline race. It is needless to recite the various combats that took place between the cats and the men. Suffice it to say, that above five hundred dead bodies were floating the next day on the River Dee, where they had been ignominiously thrown by their victors. The rest of the invading host having evacuated the town, dispersed in utter confusion, carrying with them, however, their arms from the field of battle.*

(Royal Cornwall Gazette, 23 September 1815)

Report on the Dissection of the Body of Napoleon Bonaparte

Graphic details of a post mortem carried out on the body of Napoleon was published in full by the press. Conducted in the presence of four surgeons led by principal medical officer Thomas Shortt, the team concluded that the 'heart was of natural size... the lungs were sound... there was a healthy appearance to the liver' before examining what they believed was the cause of death in the stomach:

Upon opening the abdomen the omentum was found remarkably fat, and on exposing the stomach that viscus was found the seat of extensive disease. Strong adhesions connected the whole superior surface, particularly about the pyloric extremity to the concave surface of the left lobe of the liver; and on separating these, an ulcer, which penetrated the coats of the stomach, was discovered one inch from the pylorus, sufficient to allow the passage of the little finger. The internal surface of the stomach, to nearly its whole extent, was a mass of cancerous disease or scirrhous portions advancing to cancer: this was particularly noticed near the pylorus. The cardiac extremity, for a small space near the termination of the oesophagus, was the only part appearing in a healthy state. The stomach was found nearly filled with a large quantity of fluid resembling coffee grounds.

(*London Gazette,* 7 July 1821)

The Death of General War

We have great pleasure in announcing the death of General War! This distinguished character died a few evenings ago at his late seat in France. He has left numerous offspring behind him, and immense riches, which he has bequeathed by will in the following manner: To France repose; to Great

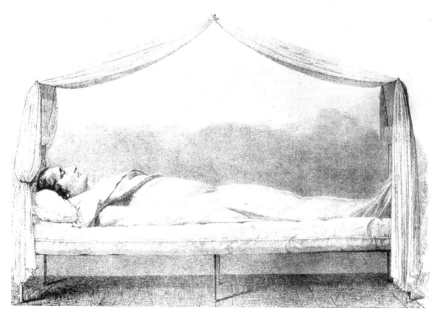

The post mortem concluded that the cause of death was stomach cancer

Britain commerce; to Austria, the whole of his beautiful estates in Italy; to the King of Prussia, formerly his very good friend and ally, the whole of his possessions in Saxony, with all the fish ponds, and little rivulets, and the right of dabbling in them as much as he pleases; as a mark of his respect for Emperor Alexander [of Russia], he has made him heir to his little establishment in Poland, with all the out houses, cattle, SLAVES, and sugar casks belonging to it, principally for the quiet and magnificent manner in which he treated the General when in Russia, and also to remunerate him for the immense expense he put himself to in fireworks at that time. While living he was the rank enemy of all Emperors, Kings and Princes, yet he was courted and even run after by many of them: however, to ease his conscience, while on his death-bed, he gave the above bequests. There is hardly an individual now existing but is, in some measure, benefitted by his death. A Codicil annexed to his will contains some trifling legacies to some persons with whom he had been in habits of intimacy: to all the Field Marshalls, Generals and superior officers, the stock of Honour and Glory acquired at Moscow, Leipsig, Salamanca, Waterloo etc., besides the grant of a Dutch principality to Wellington, and many other valuable presents to Blucher, Platoff, Hill, Winzingerode, Anglesea etc., etc., etc., - to all contractors, stock jobbers and agents, a mourning ring each; to all authors and poets, permission to write his epitaph - and to all the world, PEACE!

(*Trewman's Exeter Flying Post*, 7 December 1815)

Proud Bellerophon a Hundred Years Away

Europe enjoyed relative peace for almost a hundred years after the end of the Napoleonic Wars, before the world was plunged into the Great War. The British press made comparisons between the exploits of Bonaparte and the expansionist ambitions of Kaiser Wilhelm of Germany. The following poem, written in 1915, questions the thoughts of a WWI soldier in Torquay, gazing out from the Royal Terrace Gardens (also known as Rock Walk) across Torbay to Berry Head where the *Bellerophon* had anchored with her prized passenger a century earlier:

Napoleon looks down on the
ambitions of Kaiser Wilhelm

Dear Soldier on the Rocky Walk,
As lonely as can be,
What is it you are thinking of,
Thinking so weightily?
What are the sights that meet your eye
Gazing across the sea?
A penny, Soldier, for your thoughts.
Oh tell your thoughts to me.
In fancy's golden regions,
D'you see across the Bay,
The bows of proud Bellerophon
A hundred years away?
And the caged lion walking,
Along his narrow trek,
And with the sailors talking
Upon that gallant deck?

* * *

Or does your kind heart journey
Where childhood's scenes were laid,
To some far county
Where waits some loving maid?
A penny, Soldier, for your thoughts.
I will not be gainsaid.

* * *

'What do I think? Mostly naught.
Sometimes of the old mother.
Girls? Nay, the girls don't bother me
I gives 'em a wink and lets 'em be.
One girl's darned like another.
So I wink and they wink, and that's, I think
The lot they'll get from me awhile.
For a kiss costs more than a passing smile,

And I scarcely give the girls a thought.
But it's company, like, when the day is done.
And the boys march off for a bit o' fun,
To watch the waves as they rise and fall,
And sometimes I seem to hear them call
When the light flashes out by Berry Head.
But I bain't really thinking of nothing at all,
So it's little you get for your penny', he said,
'But, if I can't think, I can jolly well fight,
And I'll do my bit (you may bet) all right',
Ah, Soldier, the thinkers will bless you.
Goodnight.
A Colloquy by CE Sharpley,
Torquay Times, 20 August 1915

Remembering Napoleon

At the village of Downham, Essex, is Mrs Sarah Brooks, the only living person in England, who ever saw Napoleon. Although in her 104th year, she still enjoys excellent health. Mrs Brooks was born on March 2nd 1812, at Plymouth. She was thus nearly three and a half years old when Napoleon was taken a captive in the Bellerophon *into Plymouth Sound from Torbay. Her father rowed her, with a party of friends, to see the vessel.*
(*Torquay Directory*, 21 July 1915)

Bicentenary of Waterloo

Two hundred years on from the Battle of Waterloo, it is strange to reflect that more biographies, poems and folk songs have been written in this country about the vanquished Napoleon Bonaparte than the victor, the Duke of Wellington, who like his foe, also entered politics, serving as Prime Minister of Great Britain. Popular interest stirred by the nation's enemy during his sojourn in England has continued unabated and was prophesied in the following folk song that emerged in the wake of the fallen emperor's death, rightly asserting that 'his name will never be forgot':

Grand Conversation on Napoleon

It was over that wild beaten track 'twas said a friend of Bonaparte's
Did pace the sands and the lofty rocks of St Helena's shore,
And the wind it blew a hurricane, the lightning fierce around did dart,
The seagulls were a-shrieking and the waves around did roar.
Ah hush, rude winds, the stranger cried, while I range the spot
Where alas the gallant hero did his weary eyelids close.
And though at peace his limbs do rest, his name will never be forgot.
This grand conversation on Napoleon arose.

Oh alas, he cried, why England did you persecute that hero bold?
Much better had you slain him on the plains of Waterloo.
For Napoleon he was a friend to heroes all, both young and old,
He caused the money for to fly wherever he did go.
When plans were forming night and day, the bold commander to betray,
He said, I'll go to Moscow and there I'll ease my woes.
And if fortune smiles on me that day, then all the world shall me obey,
This grand conversation on Napoleon arose.

Oh his men in thousands then did rise to conquer Moscow by surprise,
He led his troops across the Alps oppressed by frost and snow,
And being near the Russian land, he then began to open his eyes,
For Moscow was a-blazing and the men drove to and fro.
Napoleon dauntless viewed the plain and then in anguish at the same,
He cried, 'Retreat me gallant men, for time so swiftly goes'.
Ah what thousands died in that retreat, some forced their horses for to eat.
This grand conversation on Napoleon arose.

At Waterloo they bravely fought, commanded by this Bonaparte,
Field Marshall Ney did him betray, but he was bribed by gold.
And when Blucher led the Prussians, it nearly broke Napoleon's heart.
He cried, my thirty thousand men are lost, and I am sold
He viewed the plain and cried, all's lost, and then his favourite charger crossed,
The plain was in confusion with blood and dying woes.

Wellington issues orders to his officers on the battlefield

And the bunch of roses did advance and boldly entered into France.
This grand conversation on Napoleon arose.

Oh, this Bonaparte was planned to be a prisoner across the sea,
The rocks of St Helena, oh, it was his final spot.
And as a prisoner there to be till death did end his misery.
His son soon followed to the tomb: it was an awful plot.
And long enough have they been dead, the blast of war around us spread,
And may our shipping float again to face the daring foes.
And now my boys when honour calls we'll boldly mount those wooden walls.
This grand conversation on Napoleon arose.

Bibliography & Sources

Ashton, John. *English Caricature and Satire on Napoleon I*, London, Chatto & Windus 1884

Baring Gould, Sabine. *The Life of Napoleon Bonaparte*, London, Methuen & Co, 1897

Bowerbank, John. *An Extract From a Journal Kept On Board HMS* Bellerophon. London, Whittingham & Arliss; F.C. & J. Rivington, 1815

Broadley, Alexander Meyrick. *Napoleon in Caricature 1795-1821*, London, John Lane 1911

Cordingly, David. Billy Ruffian, London, Bloomsbury Publishing, 2003

Duhamel, Jean. *Fifty Days in England: Napoleon in England*, London, Rupert Harte-Davis, 1969

Home, George. *Memoirs of an Aristocrat, and Reminiscences of the Emperor Napoleon. By a Midshipman of the* Bellerophon. London: Whittaker & Co., Ave Maria Lane, and Bell and Bradfute, Edinburgh. 1838.

Martineau, Gilbert. *Napoleon Surrenders*, London, John Murray Ltd, 1971

Scott, Sir Walter. *The Life of Napoleon Buonaparte*, Emperor of the French Edinburgh Cadwell & Co., 1827

Tovell, Freeman M. *Napoleon and his Fellow Passengers*, London, Cassell & Co., 1908

White, H.T. *A History of Torquay*, Torquay 1878

Newspapers and Periodicals:
Bailey's Magazine, Blackwood's Edinburgh Magazine, The Courier, Flindell's Western Luminary, Lancaster Gazette & General Advertiser, London Gazette, Morning Chronicle, Morning Herald, Morning Post, Plymouth Dock Telegraph, Royal Cornwall Gazette, Falmouth Packet & Plymouth Journal, St James Chronicle, The News, The Times, Torquay Directory, Torquay Times, Trewman's Exeter Flying Post.

Website Sources:
BBC History: bbc.co.uk/history
Bytes of Torbay's Past: torbytes.co.uk
Internet Archive: archive.org
Nineteenth Century Newspapers: gale.cengage.co.uk
Times Digital Archive: gale.cengage.co.uk